Let your dreams lead,
happiness will follow.

Rusty

YOU SHOULD ONLY HAVE TO GET RICH ONCE

YOU SHOULD ONLY HAVE TO GET RICH ONCE

How to Avoid Toxic Financial Advice
and Focus on What Really Matters

Russell E. Holcombe

EMERALD
BOOK CO.

Published by Emerald Book Company
Austin, TX
www.emeraldbookcompany.com

Copyright ©2012 Russell Holcombe

All rights reserved.

No part of this book may be reproduced, stored in a retrieval system, or transmitted by any means, electronic, mechanical, photocopying, recording, or otherwise, without written permission from the copyright holder.

Distributed by Emerald Book Company

For ordering information or special discounts for bulk purchases, please contact Emerald Book Company at PO Box 91869, Austin, TX 78709, 512.891.6100.

Design and composition by Greenleaf Book Group LLC
Cover design by Sergio Velez
Illustrations by Jessica Hagy, Sergio Velez, and Craig Barrington Howarth II

Publisher's Cataloging-in-Publication Data
(Prepared by The Donohue Group, Inc.)
Holcombe, Russell E.
    You should only have to get rich once : how to avoid toxic financial advice and focus on what really matters / Russell E. Holcombe. — 1st ed.
    p. : ill., charts ; cm.
    ISBN: 978-1-937110-14-7
    1. Finance, Personal—Planning. 2. Investments—Planning. 3. Wealth—Management. I. Title.
HG179 .H65 2012
332.02401   2011932969

Part of the Tree Neutral® program, which offsets the number of trees consumed in the production and printing of this book by taking proactive steps, such as planting trees in direct proportion to the number of trees used: www.treeneutral.com.

TreeNeutral

Printed in the United States of America on acid-free paper

12 13 14 15 16   10 9 8 7 6 5 4 3 2 1

First Edition

Contents

NOTE TO READER

The stories in this book were inspired by a lifetime of experiences. Wall Street uses story to make us feel and act a certain way. We have deliberately used the same technique to make you feel and act in your self-interest. Please proceed with caution. You will never look at wealth or your wealth manager the same way again.

Preface

So I'm sitting in the lobby of the Ritz-Carlton in Atlanta—ground zero for the financial factory in the Southeast. Within a one-mile radius, 95 percent of the participants in the warfare on wealth have their offices. The delicate ballet begins every morning around 7:00 a.m. This is when brokers and financial advisors get ready to pitch another investment. They march into the glistening towers. Game on.

From where I sit, I can see one distinguished older gentleman wearing a colorful Tommy Bahama shirt and linen pants. He is surrounded by three very polished money managers from the financial factory. The managers hand out beautiful eye candy for the wealthy man to read. The man looks at the colorful charts, financial tables, and future projections. A hollow yet optimistic gaze crawls onto his face. It's clear he doesn't understand what is in front of him, but he's happy anyway. Potential profit is the purest aphrodisiac.

From a distance, I can tell the brochures are convincing the man to let the managers invest his money. Their presentation makes it look easy. I want so badly to yell, "Run while you still have a chance!" There's nothing wrong with picking up a $20 bill lying on the sidewalk—right? For the money managers, this man represented that $20 bill.

Occasionally, I'll grab the financial newspapers and read about the latest in financial chicanery. It was during one of these morning reflections I decided to write this book.

The process of writing this book has been a long one. It began long before the latest market collapse. The deception of Wall Street was not a mystery to me; every new product created to generate a fee is so predictable. Auction-rate securities, hedge funds, indexed annuities, and exchange-traded funds were created to make investing seem easy while generating fees. I am never surprised when these products fail to perform as promised. But I was clueless about why smart clients continue to tread a committed path toward financial destruction.

It made no sense to me how people smart enough to accumulate wealth were so helpless to defend themselves against toxic financial advice. To get to the bottom of this I needed to understand more than finance. I began reading every book I could find on psychology, behavior, intuition, sales, branding, and marketing. I wanted to figure out how we think. It soon became very clear to me how easily the financial factory can brainwash the brightest minds. Optical illusions provide unique insight into why this is so. Look at the illustration below. Which line is longer?

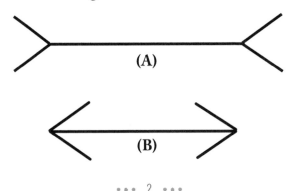

The Müller-Lyer illusion deceives each person in the exact same way, regardless of IQ, education, or profession. Both lines are the same length.

Similarly, the financial factory leverages our default tendency to consistently make mistakes. The factory understands our logical lust for patterns, our desire for certainty, and our inherent optimism about the future.

Humans are fundamentally seekers. We seek those claiming to have solved life's randomness. In our zeal for answers, we forget—psychics never win lotteries. Financial companies with a vested interest in our assets appeal to our "seeker psychology." They give us what we want, something to believe in. Awareness is the most effective tool for deleveraging their advantage. While greater awareness won't solve every problem, it will provide the telescope to see the problem as it rounds the corner.

Once you read this book, you'll never look at your wealth the same way again.

"The life of every man is a diary in which he means to write one story and writes another. And his humblest hour is when he compares the volume as it is with what he vowed to make it."

—James M. Barrie

Introduction

Imagine entering the New York City Marathon only to find they've made a key change. This year there will be no finish line. How will you train for such a race? You couldn't. How will you know if you'd won the race? You wouldn't. Better yet, how long would you watch your favorite sporting event if the goal was for both teams to play ad infinitum? No winners, no losers. Seems ridiculous doesn't it? Did you know this accurately represents the traditional financial planning model? Always playing, never winning. Has a financial advisor ever told you it was time to stop investing because you won the race?

The stories in this book reflect experiences I've struggled with over the last eighteen years as I witnessed people implode financially. People who relied on financial philosophies that simply did not work.

I've always felt the motto "To Protect and Serve" should represent financial advisors as much as it does law enforcement. Unfortunately, there are very few people in my industry who live by this philosophy. Instead, many promote a very different belief system, one dangerous to a person with wealth, especially wealth not easily replaceable. This belief system says, "You can never have enough money," which sounds good at first, until you really think about it. Life is short and unpredictable. Wealthy people must think differently to protect their lifestyle. And the current system of financial planning is not designed to do this.

OUR COMMON CONNECTION

We all love the underdog. It inspires us when the unlikely emerges victorious. We connect with the little guy who steps in the ring to fight the champion. Underdogs struggle against all odds to keep their quest for victory alive. They want to see what it feels like to win, just once. This touches a place deep inside us because we all struggle to keep our passions, our dreams, alive. No matter how successful you are, there is an underdog in you. The dream you keep hidden well out of reach of pessimism and discouragement.

No one believes in your dream like you do. No one encourages your passion to grow. People will listen courteously, but few think it will become a reality. After all, they buried their dreams long ago and softly believe you should do the same. You are encouraged to get in line and follow the script. But you know there's more—you feel it, you sense it.

OUR COMMON ENEMY

The financial system (I call it the financial factory) is the greatest distraction keeping you from following your dream. The system promotes its agenda and sacrifices yours. Don't let it happen. Pull for your underdog. Pull for your passion. But be aware of one thing: To break from conformity and build the life you want will require a resolute attitude. It will not be easy.

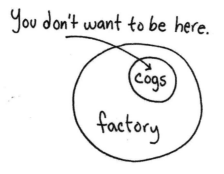

Staying wealthy isn't easy, because there are thousands of well-funded private wealth managers in major institutions across the country. Most are marketed very well. The commercials are slick and their brochures shine. This is designed to strategically pull on the emotional extremes of fear and greed. It is easy to assume that traditional wealth advisors have elevated insights qualifying them to recommend what is right for your money. In reality, traditional wealth divisions are simply populated with better-looking, better-dressing, and slightly more articulate salespeople—salespeople who advise wealthy clients to buy financial products that may or may not be best. These products range from vanilla to the exotic, but they all have one thing in common: They keep you investing.

When the latest product fails, new financial products are created out of thin air. These products come with great stories attached and promote the potential for wealth creation. But selling the benefit of more wealth to someone who has wealth is like selling water to a fish. It doesn't make sense.

In frank terms, private wealth divisions are sophisticated boiler rooms—places where stockbrokers push worthless securities on gullible clients. It is hard to notice this when you are sitting at a $50,000 conference table and listening to an advisor who's wearing a $5,000 suit. Advice can seem as valuable as the surroundings in which it is given. The irony is bad advice often comes in pristine packaging.

THE TRADITIONAL FINANCIAL PLANNING MODEL

To say the traditional financial planning model is broken implies that at some point in time it was operating effectively, and maybe it was. Today it is outdated and irrelevant. All the "get to know you" interviews and feel-good moments are designed to get you to do one thing—invest in their financial products. I see clients all the time who took huge losses in a market they should have never been in to begin with. Rarely does anyone ask the wealthy client to explain the purpose for their wealth or what means the most to them outside of a ledger balance. The "one size fits all" traditional approach to financial planning forces wealthy clients into aspirational mode. It makes them seekers of what they've already found.

Severe market volatility is like an alarm clock. It wakes us up and shines a spotlight on the problems with traditional investment advice. Many traditional financial advisors really believe they are doing good for you. Many are sincere. Unfortunately, they are sincerely wrong. Of all clients, the wealthy client has the most to lose using traditional financial planning because this approach is not designed to protect and serve. It is only designed to keep you playing.

The good news for you is that the innovative financial planning model I explain in this book has found its tipping point. (Malcolm Gladwell describes a tipping point as the "magic moment when an idea, trend, or social behavior crosses a threshold, tips, and spreads like wildfire.") I arrive at this conclusion because wealthy clients have endured bad markets before, the dollar has fallen before, and corporate malfeasants have always been with us. But something has changed this time.

We discovered how regal firms have forced people into the generic, plaster-like model called "client." With little to no fore-thought about the consequences, financial advisors rounded up wealthy clients like herds of cattle under the deceptive title of private wealth management. These firms allowed computer software pro-grams and mathematicians to take the place of reality and emotions. They forgot about life, and what life does to inflexible plans. We are not computer models who don't feel the pinch of a 30 percent decline. The computer doesn't suffer when it takes you a decade to get your money back, if you get it back at all.

In my years of advising, I've been very lucky to be around people who truly understand wealth. They know wealth is not about yachts, vacation homes, and other fading tangibles. True wealth is discre-tionary time. It is having the resources to follow your dreams and the confidence you can afford the best care for your loved ones. Every-thing else pales in comparison.

One missed opportunity, one disease, one diagnosis—one bad event can change everything. The market crash of 1987, the tech implosion of 1999, and the recession of 2008 were considerable events, but none of these events should have been catastrophic for the wealthy client. None of these events should have led to a massive liquidation of assets to produce cash flow. If they did, you may have needed the nudge of an insightful, dissenting voice. As I explain in this book, your finish line is your "Point of Independence" and the best thing about it is this: It's *yours*. For you, this may be a $10 million net worth with X amount in quarterly income; for another this number may be much larger or much smaller. The key is, without a goal, you can play forever, but you can never win.

This book is written for the middle-class wealthy (a term I use for individuals and families with a $2 million to $20 million net worth) who may not be able to repeat the event that created their wealth. For you, a mistake hurts. This book is for corporate executives, entrepreneurs, divorcees, widows, and trust fund babies, but the lessons here can also be applied to anyone accumulating wealth. The sources of wealth are different, but the risks are the same. When you have money, you must think differently. My hope is you will uncover nuggets of actionable wisdom in this book and gain the confidence to make better decisions. You can make better decisions for you, your family, and your future by avoiding toxic financial advice and focusing on what really matters. Stop playing a game with no finish line. It's okay to win.

CHAPTER 1

Provocateur 333

His hair is the silver of wealth. He walks with a gait that shows both confidence and vulnerability, the latter of which was held over from adolescence. As a child, David had no perceivable talents, and growing up in the Elizabeth, New Jersey, public housing projects doesn't provide much self-esteem. His frail frame was overshadowed by a noticeable limp. "Hey, Scarecrow!" was a routine dig shouted as he waited for the bus each morning. Poverty, crime, and ridicule can make for a most difficult environment. A "self-made" millionaire today, David almost always refuses to share childhood memories, except for one story.

It was early January 1957. David, along with other kids in the housing projects, prepared for school. It had been snowing for three days with three more days forecast. As an only child to a widowed mother, David felt he got more love than most kids his age, but he needed more than love on days like this. He needed warm clothes.

His mother, Miriam, usually got his clothes from the local Salvation Army long before the cold days hit, but this year inventory was sparse.

Too many families were having hard times. The postwar economy was beginning, but it would be many years before families such as David's would experience anything other than lack. In his neighborhood, all the warm items were taken. David knew asking his mom for a coat would only hurt her. She wanted to provide for him but didn't have the resources. It was either food or clothes this year.

Living with limited resources made an indelible impression on David; so did the number 333. It was burned into his memory seemingly from the time he was born. His mother repeated "333" like a religious chant throughout the house. It was the default answer to most questions. This number represented the exact amount of money they had to live off of each month; it was their cash flow, their lifeline. No matter the need, if it didn't fit within $333, they did without.

On that snowy January morning, David stood at the school bus stop in a sweater more appropriate for early fall. He knew he wasn't dressed adequately but had learned to do with less without complaining. His shoes were stuffed with old newspaper collected from homes his mom cleaned. As schoolkids began to gather, one young boy asked a particularly embarrassing question: "Doesn't your mom have enough money for a coat?" David paused to gather himself before answering. Even among poor kids there was peer pressure, and a big warm coat for the winter was one of the few things they could be proud of. "She has enough," David answered with more hope than reality. "I just share it with my cousin and it's her turn to wear it today. I'll wear it tomorrow," he declared. David had no such cousin, and no such coat.

For the rest of the winter, David oscillated from excuse to excuse as kids as poor as he made fun of his worse condition. That period of his life, the winter of '57, was especially painful. There had been bad times before, but something was different this time. Maybe it was because he had just turned twelve and was becoming more aware of his family's desperate condition. He started to wonder whether this would be his life, one of lack. He spent many nights staring at the water-spotted ceiling in his room and wondering what his number would be when he grew up. Would it be 444, 555, or 777? How much money would his family have to live on?

In a small but profound way, David started to understand the importance of predictable cash flow. No matter how great or small the number was, you had to have a certain amount each month to survive. His mother never used credit. She drilled this into David with the words, "Debt is a thief and robber; it steals all you work for"—a lesson he would never forget.

Today, David is a retired businessman who describes January 1957 as if it were yesterday. The emotions are still palpable. And even with all the wealth he's attained, remnants of embarrassment from having no coat linger. When one walks into his pristine ski lodge–themed office, there's an expectation of a giant elk or deer on the wall. There is none. Instead, a beautifully carved wooden mounting over his desk reads "333." The number that provoked him to do more.

The number 333 provoked him to go to school, start a manufacturing company, and eventually become a wealthy man. Provocation is powerful. The number 333 kept him from using credit in his business dealings. When other companies were quick to expand, he was more calculated. When competitors were hiring more employees than needed, he kept a skeleton, yet efficient, staff. When business colleagues were overleveraging themselves with luxury real estate,

David instead paid for his residences in cash and carried no debt. His childhood provoked him to make better financial decisions.

Historically, a provocateur has been defined as a person who causes trouble. In reality, a provocateur is much more and can include events, environments, or even numbers pushing us into unchartered territories, territories that lie just past where we would normally be satisfied. Without positive provocation, little can be accomplished of any merit.

Encouragement is a provocateur; so is discouragement. For the religious person, faith provokes actions of persistence when others give up. A competitive drive is the provocateur for athletes who, fully fatigued, are unwilling to give up another point to their opponent. Provocateurs of all kinds can agitate us toward doing more, reaching deeper, getting up earlier, or staying up later. Provocateurs incite us to do better.

By the age of sixty-three, David had amassed a small fortune. He lives conservatively and has survived market crashes and severe economic downturns. After all, he survived these things as a child. When companies started downsizing, he was hiring. When foreclosures were high, he was buying properties at basement prices. David was provoked very early to think clearly and respect the fragility of money, long before he had any. This made him patient; this kept him wealthy.

EXPERIENCE—THE BEST ADVISOR

We owe much of what we do today to our past, good and bad. I can empathize with David in many ways.

I hated high school because I hate cliques, groups of people who reward other people because of their adaptation to an ill-conceived status quo. My high school had no windows, a horribly depressing environment. I've tried hard to think of some, but I have no positive memories of my high school experience. I grew up in Sandy Springs, Georgia (outside of Atlanta), with entrepreneurial parents who were long on ability but short on money. I learned very early the hardships involved when you have to carve your existence out of a faint idea and a desire to do better. Fueled only with passion, my parents spent years trying to make something out of themselves. They tried to give their children something to build on.

My earliest memories are of me sitting at home alone or at the office waiting endlessly as my parents worked day in and day out. I had few of the normal childhood experiences other kids enjoyed. That just wasn't my reality. I wasn't the cool guy. I was kind of quirky in that I questioned everything. I wanted to know why things were the way they were, and who said they had to be that way. Add to this a social phobia, and you come up with a lot of time to think.

I shied away from anything popular; those things just seemed trivial to me. I did play tennis until the age of fourteen and was ranked second from last in the state of Georgia. At the time I considered this a failure, but I guess one must have a tiny bit of talent to even come in last. I learned early how attracted I was to things I couldn't do. I liked a challenge. Challenges seemed substantive, something I craved.

After high school I was accepted into Southern Methodist University, another challenge I fully embraced. SMU exposed me to an entirely different environment. Between 1989 and 1993, I witnessed one of the worst recessions in Dallas, yet Highland Park, where SMU is located, was seemingly unaffected by the surrounding economy.

I witnessed individuals take full advantage of the difficulties affecting others. It was like an all-you-can-eat buffet of opportunity, and nobody was in line. This greatly affected my views on investing and risk. By the time I graduated, my grades were far from Wall Street ready. My tendency to go into areas of challenge led me to take very difficult classes. But not going to Wall Street was the best thing that ever happened to me. At SMU I exposed myself to finance, but also to British dramatic comedy and a music class called The Art of Listening. I'm tone deaf. Without a good GPA, your Wall Street application becomes a comedy in and of itself. But then a weird, fortunate thing happened.

I must have written a hell of an essay, because for some reason I was accepted into the honors portfolio management program at SMU. We managed $2 million of the university endowment. We were also exposed to insightful money management firms who didn't come out of the Wall Street factory. This company questioned everything, made no predictions, and today they remain some of the most successful institutional advisors in the world. I started to feel at home. This was the time when seeds of skepticism toward the "financial experts" were firmly planted in me. The worst financial failures ever recorded in history have come at the hands of some of the smartest people in the world, people who concentrated on what they knew but who never spent time studying areas or disciplines for which they had no talent. Confidence without vulnerability is a toxic combination.

When I reflect on how I got to where I am today, several things come to mind. Some events are clearly attached to a certain result, but there are others with no direct relationship to anything. They are random. These events exist without prerequisite. They are pure chance.

PURE CHANCE

There is nothing more random than being born into the right family. Chance is like an invisible chain; it is connected, but nobody knows where. Many of you reading this can attest to the fragility of chance. At some point in all of our lives, we've thought of how things would have changed if we'd missed one meeting or grown up a few blocks down from where we did.

There are an estimated 1,000,000 people worldwide with a net worth in excess of $10 million; 300,000 of these 1,000,000 live in the United States.[1] Wealth is rare.

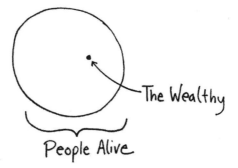

In Malcolm Gladwell's book *Outliers*, he details why our explanations of success just don't work. He writes, "The tallest oak in the forest is the tallest not just because it grew from the hardiest acorn; it is also the tallest because no other trees blocked its sunlight, the soil around it was deep and rich, no rabbit chewed through its bark as a sapling, and no lumberjack cut it down before it matured."

Life has a lot more to do with what we don't know than what

---

1   Capgemini *World Wealth Report 2009*.

we do. The tender trajectory of our destiny is mysterious. My very existence bears this out.

My mom grew up in a small tobacco-farming town outside of Bowling Green, Kentucky. People go to Bowling Green only to visit the Corvette factory. It is a pretty dry place. She had three choices: work on the farm, work in a fast food restaurant, or leave Bowling Green altogether. She left. On the other hand, my dad grew up in the Bronx, and very few people go to the Bronx to visit anything.

Graduating high school at sixteen, Dad left New York to attend Georgia Tech. By pure chance, along came the Cuban missile crisis. He was called into military service at twenty-two and spent the next two years in a submarine. The Vietnam War was escalating, but Dad could terminate enlistment if he went back to school. He quickly enrolled at Georgia State University. And coming from a submarine in the Atlantic, he meets a young pretty girl on the GSU campus, and here I am, all by chance.

THE GUY WHO COULD FIX ANYTHING

My dad comes from David's generation. He is probably much too smart for his own good. You know, the type of person who can't get his pants on correctly but has an incredibly sharp mind. My dad developed a stellar reputation in Atlanta, Georgia. If something was broken and nobody knew how to fix it, they came to him. He was the guy who could right the ship.

His early days in business actually began at the IRS. He carried a badge. He was trained to audit bad situations and find a way to get the government paid. He gained invaluable experience learning how to find money in the worst circumstances. But he wasn't always successful; he jokes about the time the IRS made him visit a federal prison in Atlanta to collect taxes from a convicted money launderer. I guess some situations are beyond fixing.

He left the IRS and started working for an insurance company in the retirement plan division. In 1974, the Employment Retirement Income and Security Act (ERISA) became law and the insurance company exited the business. He took it over and my parents instantaneously became entrepreneurs. I was four.

ERISA was new, the laws were complex, and failure to live by the new rules was expensive. The early days were full of badly constructed retirement plans, sold mostly to doctors. This was largely because doctors were the only people making real money. They were easy targets for the financial factory. All the salespeople had to do was find a hospital and wander the halls. You'd randomly bump into money. Dad was the "financial M.D." saving doctors and other professionals from bad situations. He patched financial wounds.

My father's work was the provocateur for what I am doing today, helping the wealthy client stay wealthy. I studied failures and, to a certain extent, lived these failures vicariously. I saw firsthand how bad financial products can damage very intelligent, unsuspecting clients. As a kid, I also gained a healthy respect for the randomness of life. Where you are born, what city you grew up in, and who your friends are can have as much to do with your future success as any degree or training.

MY OFFICIAL ARRIVAL

I arrived on the investment scene in 1993 at the end of the oil and real estate crash in Dallas, Texas. This was the beginning of a huge boom/bust period. The sources of wealth were all the same—right place, right time, right vision, and hard work. Millions were made, and then millions were lost. *What is happening to these people?* I asked myself. Did they not know how fortunate they were? So my journey to educate began. Once you have money, your focus must change. Why? Because wealth is rare. Nobody can predict which event will cause wealth to appear. But when it does, don't let money and the pursuit of more pull you away from common sense.

IMAGINATION PROMOTES SAFETY

Many of the problems I see today are a result of unimaginative thinking. People who have never experienced what David or my dad experienced have a difficult time imagining real poverty. Clients like these have never lost everything. Yes, they've seen lean times, but for the most part, they have yet to experience intense financial trauma.

Granted, it's difficult to imagine what you've never seen. It's hard to imagine triple bypass surgery when the worse you've experienced is a headache. At first, many of the suggestions I make to wealthy clients can seem paranoid. But in order to maintain your wealth, you must create experiences in your mind to test the boundaries of your emotions. That is precisely what flight simulators do for pilots. Simulators take pilots to the edge of their emotional and psychological limits in an effort to expand their understanding. Trauma trains instincts. The same must be done when thinking of what can happen to your wealth. It takes confidence to acquire wealth, but a reasonable dose of paranoia is needed to keep it. Remember, the wealthy person has much less to gain from making more money.

I know, it's kind of a weird approach because, when making

a financial decision, you already have processed the good part by default. People who purchase a lotto ticket buy a dream for $1. They ignore the 99.999 percent chance of losing. But this type of thinking is also practiced by those who've already won a kind of personal lottery. I refer to the wealthy.

Thinking about all the good things that can happen is deeper than it seems at first glance. This is because when you have money the good side has less room to get better. Will Bill Gates or Warren Buffett change lifestyles once they earn another billion? Of course not. For them, another billion is an arbitrary ledger entry. Let's look at an example more relevant to your finances.

DOES MORE MAKE YOU HAPPIER?

Imagine James, a forty-five-year-old investor with $100,000 in investable assets. He is desperately looking to put this money to work for the next fifteen years. His objective is to turn this money into $1 million for his retirement fund. While this objective is lofty, it is far from being impossible. Let's say with this $100,000 he purchased 12,500 shares of Apple stock in 1995. By 2010, fifteen years later, the $100,000 would be worth $2.5 million, $1.5 million more than he originally desired.

With this money, James can pay off a $300,000 mortgage. He already owns his vehicles and a small boat, and his monthly monetary needs (health care, insurance payments, food, utilities, taxes, etc.) are $4,500. If he lets his $2.2 million sit in cash, James could live stress-free for thirty-seven years without ever worrying about earning money. For him, this defines "all the good things that could happen." But what if you change the numbers in this scenario?

James is still forty-five and symbolizes the middle-class wealthy, with $5 million in liquid assets. His home is paid for, and he seeks to spend more time with his children while pursuing a passion for painting portraits of famous people. While investing in Apple stock would have substantially increased his net worth, it would not create anything in his life he didn't already have. Think about it. Yes, he could buy a second house and a bigger boat, but his quality of life would not change with investing this money. His life would increase in "having things," but the quality of his life would change little. In fact, one could convincingly argue that more things generate more headaches and more management issues. But who will tell James to stay out of the market, enjoy his life, and follow his passions?

AN OUTSIDER ON THE INSIDE

Let me be abundantly clear: I make my living managing money. At a glance, this fact seems to position me as the most unlikely person to criticize and disassemble the financial services industry. Simply put, I see things a little differently than many of my colleagues. My true value to my clients is coaching, my nudging them to go where they know they should go, and do what they already know they should do. I don't create destinations; I point to them and say, "Go!"

Yes, many times in this book I speak about staying out of the markets, but I am not against investing. I invest every day on behalf of my clients. I am, however, vehemently opposed to over-investing and under-thinking. I frequently discuss the erroneous financial planning model practiced by many advisors, yet I am not against seeking financial advice. I am not opposed to buying stocks, only buying stocks for the wrong reasons. These positions were birthed out of watching more financial train wrecks than I can count. Helping you avoid one is my personal passion.

One of my favorite words in the English language is "appropriate." It is one of my favorites because it is descriptive. It needs no explanation. When you find what makes you happy, when you find what gives purpose to your life, it becomes easy to see what is most appropriate for you. My brother is a perfect example of this. Brian enrolled at Georgia Tech and, as prestigious as this university is, it didn't fit. Why? He's an artist. He can perceive distinctions nobody else can. Art and engineering are not on the same planet. He was miserable.

FINDING WHAT'S APPROPRIATE FOR YOU

Brian eventually found his way into an art program at Georgia State University. He quickly exhausted their resources and transferred to the Art Institute of Chicago. He found his home. The school is located in the basement of the Art Institute and the kids have amazing resources and eccentricities. Graduation looked more like a costume party, and the commencement speaker danced for thirty minutes before advising the students not to waste their time trying to figure out life, telling them instead to just have sex often. Brian returned to Atlanta, and he opened one of the first galleries in the city dedicated to conceptual art. Atlanta is not an art town, but he quickly made a name for himself. He found artists in the most unlikely places, and many now have pieces in the finest museums in New York. Finding what is appropriate for you may take a while, but it's worth every second.

Many people love camping because it makes them feel one with nature. The activity generally takes place in beautiful mountainous or wooded surroundings. When experienced campers pack for the trip, they instinctually understand what to take and what to leave home.

Survival items, food, and warm clothing are all appropriate because their destination is clearly defined. They don't load up the car with flat screen televisions, desktop computers, or anything that contradicts the simplicity of a camping environment. These things wouldn't be appropriate. I coach my clients using this very principle. Spending time defining exactly where you plan to go is the first step toward understanding what is appropriate for your journey. Unfortunately, most people go through life traveling without ever defining their destination.

We all have different camping trips. For some, the "camping trip" is raising their family, opening a bar, starting a boutique, traveling to every baseball park in the United States, climbing the tallest mountain, or building a business. Every person reading this has a dream. Whether you choose to make it a reality is up to you.

The financial factory is oblivious to your dream but very aware of its own. The factory assumes all of our camping trips are exactly the same. It is a devastating philosophy for people who know what makes them happy.

As your options expand, so does the time it takes to make the right choices. But when you're engulfed in analyzing your options, it becomes easy to forget what truly matters. It is a toxic cycle.

You need a financial canary, one to keep you from going so deep into the mine you forget how the sunshine feels. You need a positive provocateur.

CHAPTER 2

Peruvian Lessons for Good Financial Planning

Lifting the hospital sheet, Carmen Villanueva got the shock of her life. Her father's right foot was gone. Her shock was second only to her confusion. She looked, looked again, and looked a third time to confirm her discovery. Her father, Jorge Villanueva, went to the hospital with an ulcer on his foot, the left one. Gangrene had set in and the doctors made the decision to amputate.

Surgery was scheduled. On the morning of January 5, 2010, a team of surgeons and nurses rolled Mr. Villanueva into an operating room at Alberto Sabogal Hospital in Callao, Peru, put him under anesthesia, lifted the sheet, and cut off his healthy foot, leaving the gangrenous foot still attached to his body.

It wasn't until his daughter arrived that the medical staff learned the sick foot was still there. The surgeons hadn't noticed. A second surgery was scheduled, this time removing the correct foot. Today, Mr. Villanueva has no feet.

There are many disturbing elements in this story, but the first question a fan of logic would ask is "How did this happen?" The simple answer is: bad planning.

A room full of physicians and trained nurses were too committed to the general process to notice the specifics of the patient in front of them. One less assumption, one astute observation, one double-check would have saved Mr. Villanueva from the life he now has.

Any time a template-like process overcomes an obsession with getting it right, bad things can happen.

Unfortunately, this mind-boggling mistake is not uncommon. Arthur Newmark, M.D., runs a website where he reports on "wrong side surgeries."[2] Newmark exposes medical oversights that are difficult to comprehend. His reports include doctors in Minneapolis removing the wrong kidney, California doctors operating on the wrong knee, a neurosurgeon operating on the wrong side of a brain, and even a physician who mistakenly did one procedure he was scheduled to do on another patient—twice!

Recognizing the need for building a safer health system, many hospitals have hired consultants to double-check operating room procedures. In 2000, a very important book revealed to the public what many medical professionals already knew. *To Err Is Human: Building a Safer Health System* reports that nearly 100,000 people die each year from such errors. The book asserts that the problem is not bad people but a bad system.

The wealthy client is not unlike Mr. Villanueva. The client sits in front of a professional with a perfectly good net worth. It need not be touched. But somehow, somewhere in the process a financial

2   http://philadelphialawyer.info/wrong-side-surgery.html.

template is forced to affect the whole when it should have touched only a small portion. This can result in the client's wealth being amputated. And just like amputating the wrong foot, recovering is not an option; the only thing left to do is adapt. Clients must simply learn to live without the money they had.

One of the few professions that have taken human error seriously is aviation. The FAA reverse engineers every tragedy in an effort to avoid repeat accidents. The investment world has a thing or two to learn from their process.

SYNCHRONIZED

On Christmas Eve 2010, I picked up a book called *Designers Don't Read* by Austin Howe. Not sure where I found the book, but I loved the title, so I ordered it. In the first sentence of the second chapter, the author says every design studio in America speaks with exactly the same voice. That one statement was like a wake-up call for what has been bothering me so much about my industry. Everyone sounds the same. In the summer of 2009, I had an intern look at the list of the top financial advisors in the United States, each of which is profiled each year by *Wealth Manager* magazine. With this information he was to review the websites of the top 400. I asked him to let me know if any of them sounded unique. We were both soundly disappointed with the results.

Out of more than 400 websites, only one of them seemed to get it. Most used words like *independent, holistic, objective, comprehensive, proprietary, individual, comfort,* and *security.* Of course they promote all these things. But value is in reducing the unknown, not stating the obvious. A grocery store's main advertisement shouldn't read, "We sell food!"

COLLABORATION, ASSUMPTIONS, AND "IF"

Establishing a good financial plan should be a highly collaborative process—one that uncovers the hidden. You, the holder of wealth, must lay out your dreams and aspirations. The architect, the financial advisor, should expose the flaws, the hurdles, and the opportunities and collaboratively build a vision of you on paper. Your plan should be a very simple, six- to ten-page document illustrating your purpose, the proper steps to advance this purpose, and potential potholes along the way. It must be solely based on *you*. When looking for a financial advisor, keep in mind the following information: The factory financial plan

- Assumes you need more money
- Assumes an investment product will solve your problems
- Assumes projections are real

If you push back on these assumptions, the financial planner quickly recites accepted clichés. For instance, maybe your advisor told you cash was a bad investment because of "inflation risk." Next, you heard, "traditionally the market returns 8 to 12 percent per year when averaged, so you should stay invested." This convinced you to stay in and watch as you lost 30 percent. Remember that cash, too, is an investment—an investment in peace.

I don't want my clients to wait for their money to return. And the best way for this to happen is to reduce the probability of them losing their money in the first place. False prediction is dangerous. It creates confidence instead of caution.

Good dialogue with your advisor builds scenarios around "What happens if?" It acknowledges an economy of chance. For those of you seeking a simple solution, understand that "if" cannot be quantified; there is no equation that describes it. Unfortunately, the "What happens if?" approach is unique. But in the end, understanding the unpredictability of life can save years of unnecessary financial recovery.

A client with a company pension paying her $80,000 a year has no risk unless her company goes bankrupt. Unfortunately, there is no applicable mathematical formula to determine "if" bankruptcy will occur. There is no algorithm for saying it's going to go to 50 percent bankrupt or 30 percent bankrupt in so many years. It's an all-or-nothing deal. Financial plans must lean into this unlikely possibility and try to protect against its potential results.

This clearly is a different approach. Those who decide to embrace this new line of thinking will need a few tools before embarking on the journey.

You must

- Be honest with yourself

- Be willing to focus on what you can control

- Be willing to ignore financial predictions

- Be willing to adapt to new information

- Be willing to stress-test your assumptions

A PREDICTION EXERCISE

The assignment below highlights the randomness of the journey before you.

First, go grab a handful of note cards and a Sharpie . . . I'll wait.

Second, write down your answers to the following questions:

- What will you be doing professionally in five years?

- Will you be married, single, or divorced in five years?

- Where will the stock market be in five years?

- What will interest rates be in five years?

- What will be inflation rates in five years?

- What will your financial status be in five years?

Take your time and be as comprehensive as possible. Expand your thinking, expand your answers. The more honest you are with your expectations, the more powerful this will become.

Third, once you've finished your cards, seal them in an envelope, take them to your local bank, open a safe-deposit box, and put them in it. Do not return to look at them for five years. In five years, return to the bank and unseal the envelope. How accurate were your predictions?

The most important events would have been random. All major events will have significant financial consequences. There is no way to predict the next five days, much less the next five years. So are you going to change your purpose because of what might happen? Of course not! Are you going to cancel a vacation because of what inflation might be tomorrow? I hope not. The value in this exercise is in gaining a healthy respect for the unknown, and a healthy disrespect for those who say they know.

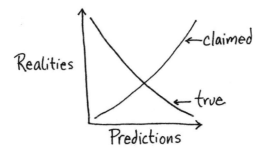

THE ENTREPRENEUR'S MIND-SET

Entrepreneurs are a very interesting group; they live in a world all their own. They see opportunities others don't see. They drop out of school to start a business. They invest when people tell them they're nuts, and they fail often without taking it personally. The problem is that most of us don't have the qualities required to be a successful entrepreneur. Why? Because we find the idea of starvation troublesome.

We like a steady paycheck. Mother Nature's survival instinct has trained us to mitigate risk. This survival instinct may be missing in entrepreneurs. They revel in starvation; they revel in famine because they know opportunity exists there. Ironically, the emotional requirements for being a good investor mimic the mentality of an entrepreneur.

Every MBA school in the land errs in thinking one can learn how to be successful in a textbook. You cannot. Good investing requires good instincts.

In addition to the five-year exercise, I use another real-time simulation to assist clients in establishing their true risk tolerance.

Take the following four scenarios. At the end of each scenario, rate how you feel emotionally about each option on a scale of 0 to 5. If you say 0, you aren't happy at all. If you say 5, you are elated. Mental simulation is critical in making this exercise as powerful as it can be. Close your eyes and really think about how you would feel before answering.

Scenario 1: You earn $100,000 each year for ten years.

Scenario 2: You earn $1,000,000 in year one and nothing for the next nine years.

Scenario 3: You earn nothing for nine years and then $1,000,000 in year ten.

Scenario 4: You make $10,000,000 in year one and then lose $1,000,000 per year for the next nine years

How did each option make you feel? Does one make you more anxious than another? The results under each scenario are identical. You have earned $1 million at the end of ten years.

According to economists (and, consequently, many financial advisors) you should be indifferent to the options presented because the outcome is the same. If you're happiest under scenario 1, you are not alone. We are wired to be the happiest with things being consistent. A steady flow of small frequent rewards leads to the highest level of comfort. Unfortunately, stock investing looks more like scenarios 2 through 4, which is the world of the entrepreneur.

Imagine toiling for nine years without earning a penny. How many of you would quit before year ten and finally get a real job? What gives entrepreneurs the stamina to last? Vision, control, and progress. When you invest in the stock market, you are investing in somebody else's vision and giving up control, and financial progress is random. Have you considered investing in yourself?

YOUR APPLE CART

For most people, there are only about four or five events that could really upset the apple cart. It isn't always death, and it isn't always disability. Sometimes life is riskier than death.

If you become disabled, and have $10 million cash, you don't have financial risk. You have other challenges, obviously, just not financial ones. And while there's nothing a financial plan can do to limit the possibility of becoming disabled, a good financial plan prepares you for the unpredictable. These types of lifestyle adjustments don't show up in a financial plan. These adjustments show up between your ears.

A good plan says: "All right, here are the four or five things that can go wrong with you. You already have money. If you die, we're sad. Everybody else still has money. If you become disabled, we're sad, but you still have the money to pay for the best medical care." So your risk is what? What are your "what if" scenarios? This is the foundation for creating a real plan with real benefits.

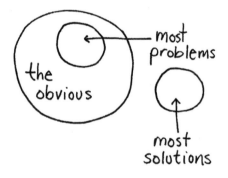

TESTING WHAT CAN GO WRONG

U.S. Secret Service professionals trained to guard the president are tested under worst-case scenarios. They are just as skilled in psychology as they are in weaponry. Their training includes intense scenarios where decisions have to be made instantly or lives are lost. Loud noises must trigger an intellectual response, not an emotional one. Their intuition about a person, place, or thing must be turned into a protective instinct. They must learn to perceive events differently. A look, an out-of-place gesture, or something picked up by the sixth sense must be instantaneously filtered into "dangerous" or "harmless" categories.

During training, Secret Service agents are isolated, tested, and emptied of whatever internal bias accompanies them to the job. An agent may turn a corner only to encounter someone holding a gun at point-blank range. This person immediately pulls the trigger. The purpose of this scenario is to train the reaction part of the brain. When successful, it slows down events. It creates time.

An NFL quarterback has about 1.5 seconds to deliver the ball to four different receivers. This, while a thousand pounds of athlete rush toward him. A first-year quarterback will always tell you it seems like they don't have enough time.

For Tom Brady, 1.5 seconds is more like 10 seconds, because he's already built mental simulations in advance. When the event happens, he knows what person is covered; he sees it instantly. He doesn't think about it; he acts. Likewise, your financial plan should be based around anticipation, not reaction.

So if I have $10 million in the bank and interest rates are 6 percent, I'm receiving $600,000 a year for the rest of my life. If T-bill rates are 6 percent, that's fine, but what happens if interest rates are 2 percent? How would you react to this reduction in cash flow? You shouldn't be surprised. You should have simulated such a reduction in yield. If it never happens, no harm, no foul. But unless you've run these simulations, you really haven't stress-tested your financial plan. And that's the real risk of relying on the current financial planning model.

• • • • •

What does all this mean? It means that, even though every financial plan is unique, I've been able to identify six elements a good financial plan must have.

A good financial plan

- Exposes purpose and advances it
- Uncovers and protects against the torpedoes that could sink your ship (given that not all can be found)
- Matches cash flow to lifestyle
- Uses Point of Independence (discussed in chapter 8) to prepare for opportunity
- Encourages investment in yourself
- Doesn't predict anything

All plans are not made equal. Plans for family vacations, diet, exercise, and marriage are great. But few will compare to the critical consequences of your financial plan.

This plan alone can set a course toward plenty or lack. Only this plan can increase the rate at which you move toward financial independence or eliminate it as a possibility altogether.

Your financial plan has little room for error. The stakes are too high. You cannot invest in a product for twenty or thirty years only to find it was the wrong product for your lifestyle. You cannot recover the time.

This requires not that you find perfection but that you be thoughtful. The quality of life you enjoy or miss has a direct relationship to the advice you receive and follow. Again, the stakes are too high to develop a plan based on advice that fits the habits and needs of your financial planner. Financial plans should be assets, not liabilities. They should be freeing, not restrictive. As we learned from Mr. Villaneuva's surgery, qualifications don't equal quality. More than understanding investing, your financial advisor must understand you.

CHAPTER 3

The True Nature of Risk

Risk is personal. It is not an intellectual construct or analysis of cor-
related and uncorrelated investments. These things are only distrac-
tions. Risk cannot be reduced to a static set of parameters; it is more
intuitive than that. Risk can never be fully contained; it is porous.
No one knows where risk is going to come from next; we only know
when it has arrived. It is the darting deer. It is the tree that just fell
around the next curve. Even though we hear about how others have
encountered unexpected risks, we give it our full attention only when
it has our name on it.

Think of it this way. There are archives of research data representing the profiles of different diseases. These diseases can then be
broken down by gender, and even further by age. You can then attain
a more granular risk profile by looking at how certain diseases tend to
affect certain dietary lifestyles. You can break it down further by your
geographical region. All of this information is edifying. But when
you stand in that cold room looking at an unfavorable X-ray while
listening to your diagnosis, those numbers don't help. It is personal.

THE PROFILE

Risk is a thief of expectations. It shocks and disappoints at the same time. The traditional approach to understanding risk has been a mathematical one. Actuaries establish catastrophic probabilities for insurance companies, and fund managers study history to hedge portfolio risk. These activities are not without merit. But let's say you hired a meteorologist consultant before building your dream home in Destin, Florida. He would come back with data on every major hurricane to hit Florida in the last 200 years, and this would be good. But does that truly define your risk of living there? It does not.

Your true risk is based on the data you *don't* have, namely, the "when." It is based on the earthquake that has never hit south Florida, those events that have no record, no history, and very little probability of occurring. You know, like the rare possibility that nearly 200 million gallons of oil would ever be spilled into the Gulf of Mexico.

Risk is the blind side. But it's more than that. To use a sports analogy, a right-handed quarterback has a perpetual risk of getting hit on his left side when he turns to throw. The left tackle reduces this risk by blocking the approaching rushers. But that is a hedge against an expected risk. Everyone knows the game; everyone knows the rushers are coming. In fact, once the defensive tackle is in place, one could argue there no longer stands a true, unpredictable risk.

IT'S COMPLICATED, SO LEAVE IT UP TO US

For the factory, claiming to understand risk is profitable. When packaged correctly, investors will pay high premiums for anyone offering elevated knowledge to reduce client investment risk. They produce complex algorithms, colorful data charts, and academics. After all, these guys are smart. These are the geniuses of the financial sector. The problem is, risk doesn't ask their permission before blowing a hole in your portfolio. Risk doesn't adhere to any preset rules. Risk marches to the beat of its own drum. It can wreak havoc at will, and without warning. Risk is rude.

Think of the millions of people who were on the edge of retirement in 2006 and 2007. They picked out a vacation cabin and bought tickets to see the grandchildren. And here comes risk. Dreams were washed away in an instant. Today, many of these individuals continue to work in order to make up for the capital they loss in an instant. That is the nature of risk. The longer you are exposed to it, the greater its chances of destroying your financial stability.

MY $100,000 OFFER TO YOU

I'll make you, the reader, a bet. I will pay you $100,000 if you stand outside for exactly five minutes and it begins to rain during that small time frame, but here are the details. I will pick the day, the location, and the time of day you will go outside. In other words, I will control all the risk. Now, if it doesn't rain during the selected time, you pay me $100,000. Great deal, isn't it! At least for me it is. But let's change a few details and watch how the risk changes dramatically.

What would happen if we changed the time you stand outside from five minutes to five hours? Well, it's still a pretty good risk on my part as long as I do my homework. What about five days? How about five weeks? Better yet, let's change it to five months. All of a sudden, you are almost guaranteed $100,000, because you'll be hard pressed to find a city in America that doesn't see a drop of rain for five months in a row. Now think about this analogy in relationship to your wealth.

When you have attained wealth, you are indoors. You are secure from the market elements that can "rain on your parade." If you decide to go outside you must understand you are exposed, and the longer you stay outside, the higher the possibility of rain. This isn't all bad, but it should make you pause. I don't tell my clients to stay indoors for the rest of their lives—that would be excessive. Instead, I believe in doing two things:

- Be patient
- Go outside with a big umbrella

Once you've done these two things, going outside takes on an entirely different meaning. Whether it rains or not, you will only get wet to a certain point. This is what proper financial planning does for you. All I am really saying is, be prepared. Your wealth allows you the opportunity to be infinitely prepared. There is no reason you should expose yourself, your family, and your lifestyle to haphazard storms forming on the horizon. Let me paraphrase how Warren Buffett explains it. He says investing is better than baseball because you can stand at the plate as long as you like. You can stand there for days or years. You don't have to swing at every pitch. You can wait for the one right over the middle of the plate. You can wait until everything is in your favor. Then and only then do you swing. That is what wealth provides, patience. Are you using it?

At the heart of understanding the nature of risk is creativity and imagination. The more scenarios you create, the more peripheral scenarios come to mind. Creativity compounds once it begins. Soon your financial planning looks more like a Tom Clancy novel than a green line in one of the smiley-faced financial commercials. The biggest risk in traditional financial planning is its lack of creativity. It lacks imagination, which is not found in formulas. It lacks an acknowledgment of the blind side.

JUST NOT SURE

Uncertainty refers to something that cannot be measured because there are no objective standards. So how does one financially plan for 9/11? You can plan to have your exposure limited to an amount you can lose and maintain your lifestyle. Let's say on Monday, September 10, you have a liquid net worth of $10 million with $1 million in the market. Your house is paid for, and you have no substantial outstanding debt. Now, if on September 12 you lose the entire $1 million, nothing in your lifestyle is affected. No one could have planned for such a catastrophic event in specific, but you could have planned for it in general. By limiting your exposure, you effectively stood in the market with a permanent umbrella covering your wealth. You could only get wet to a certain point. You weren't over-invested.

NOTHING GOOD HAPPENS ON PURPOSE

Count the events in your life that were unexpected, yet had a huge impact. Where would you be today without these events? How many came on schedule and according to plan? If you want to get an idea of someone's temperament, don't test them under ideal circumstances. Test them in severe scenarios. Likewise, if you want to look at an investment, test it under the worst assumptions. Industry failures and market crashes have provided plenty of testing material.

UNFRIENDLY SKIES

I have a client who retired from Delta Air Lines with a pension payment that would carry him and his wife for the rest of their lives. He also saved sufficiently and had $4 million in other assets. Our first job was to eliminate all debt, which left him with about $3.6 million. (I met resistance from the CPA because we were losing the worthless deduction.) He invested in stocks his whole life and had complete confidence in the markets.

I ran one scenario for him showing his cash flow if Delta filed bankruptcy. This was the one risk that could change his life. As long as Delta stayed in business, my client was financially bulletproof. He was apprehensive at first with my suggestion to invest 75 percent of his retirement assets in very safe fixed-income securities. The year was 2003, and it was uncomfortable to deviate from the very path that made him wealthy. But his life was different now. He was older and couldn't replace the $4 million with another thirty-year career flying airplanes.

In 2005, Delta filed for bankruptcy because of skyrocketing oil prices, and the qualified and non-qualified pension payments stopped immediately. I remember seeing the letter in the mail informing him that he had just received his last check. In the fall of 2008, the stock market collapsed. Many of his fellow pilots lost their retirement income, lost their retirement savings, and still had mortgage obligations.

Few people expected those two events—Delta bankruptcy and a market crash. Nobody saw that coming. In fact, those two events happening so close together was probably statistically "impossible," but reality consults with no one. Nobody was advising people with money in 2005 to avoid a risk they did not have to take. Again, life is uncertain as to when things will happen, but your bills are always on time.

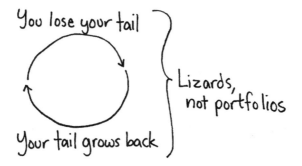

UNPREDICTABLE EVENTS

Unpredictability is an odd term. It is often misunderstood. This is because most events that can cause financial catastrophe have happened to others, thousands of times. And as we discussed in the previous chapter, when we say *unpredictable* we are really saying *untimeable*. We know 99 percent of all bad things that can or will occur; we just don't know when they will happen. Market crashes, sickness, loss of jobs, technological advances, war, divorce, and death have long histories. So why do they always surprise us? It is because trauma is hard to personalize. It is uncomfortable to put yourself in undesired circumstances, even if only hypothetically.

What makes this even more difficult is never having experienced severe financial hardship. This makes it nearly impossible to absorb lessons. Textbooks don't transfer emotions, only information. We can read about the Great Depression, 25 percent unemployment, the oil embargo of the 1970s, or the long lines of people seeking basic food items. But we still don't know what "bad" really means. We weren't there.

Once you have money, you have to think differently, you have to imagine differently from those who don't. Nothing in the factory is designed to help you engage the appropriate thought path. Think about this: People with even $1 million in assets represent a very small percentage of the population. Doesn't matter how you got it—once you have it, the rules are different. The problem is that any information you seek will encourage you to reinvest those dollars and re-expose yourself to risk: the risk of losing it, and the risk of returning to the lifestyle you led before you had money.

SLIGHTLY OFF RHYTHM

As long as the factory can keep you concentrated on the "what," you'll never focus on the "when," and being slightly off rhythm is to be totally off beat. There is no middle ground. Your financial risks must be properly framed so your energy can be efficiently utilized. In essence, anyone who pretends to have figured out market risk is like the palm reader in that little house on the side of the road. And anyone who gives credence to the self-appointed risk masters is like those who forget that psychics don't win lotteries.

Now don't get me wrong; empirical data and analysis can help clarify the general framework of investment risks, but you don't truly understand its effects until risk pays you a personal visit. Only then can you reverse-engineer the entire risk conversation and cocoon yourself against unnecessary exposure. As devastating as risk can be, without opportunity it is powerless. This must be said again: Without opportunity, risk is powerless. If you aren't standing near a tree it can't fall on you, and if you haven't over-invested you can't over-lose. The next time an advisor says the words "You'll get your money back in ten years," tell him you have your money now.

ACTORS AND RISK MANAGERS

What's the difference between actors and risk managers? Not to be harsh, but at least we know actors are playing a part. We don't expect Tom Hanks to sound like Forrest Gump in real life. Yet, we can fully appreciate his ability to take on an assumed role. He convinces us, if only for two hours, of something we know isn't true. And even more amazing, we don't feel lied to. We feel enriched. Risk managers, on the other hand, aren't supposed to be acting. In theory, they control financial risk. They tame negative potential. Most are paid handsomely to reduce the consequences of undesirable market movement. Did I mention this is theory?

The problem is that risk managers rarely understand risk. I didn't say they don't understand finance; many of them do. As I mention several times in this book, true risk isn't what has happened, it is what has not. Preparing for a market crash based on the last crash is like assuming a second car accident will not only happen at the same spot as the first but will involve the same two drivers as well. Seems ironic, but risk management divisions did little to mitigate the financial carnage of 2008–2009. They likely made it worse.

THE PURPOSE DRIVEN ACCOUNT

According to *Publishers Weekly*, the best-selling hardback book in American history is called *The Purpose Driven Life*. Its author, Rick Warren, is founder of Saddleback Church in Southern California.

The book has sold more than 30 million copies worldwide. Its content created a transformation for people seeking personal purpose in an impersonal world. The idea stuck. But there is another sticky idea on the horizon.

I call it the "Purpose Driven Account." Wealthy clients have grown weary of taking three steps forward only to suffer four steps backward. They are frustrated with being forced into investments that don't fit their reality. They are not the aspirational; they already have wealth. But most are forced into an investment philosophy made for a very different client.

I cannot count the number of times I've sat and listened to wealthy clients recount their financial wounds. These clients were never asked to articulate the true purpose of their wealth. Besides taking care of family or running a business, what else do you believe you were put here on earth to do? Only you can answer that.

The questions every wealthy person should be asked are these: What activity, cause, hobby, or initiative would you undertake if your account balance was $1 million to $10 million? What is your passion? What has been tugging on you for decades but you've found a way to ignore it? What jumps to mind right now as you read this?

When you clearly define your passion, your life takes on purpose. It frees you to follow your inner fire, whatever that fire is. Once you know this passion, your investments, your business, and your time all revolve around it. I know, I know—this concept isn't sexy, and the financial industry would laugh at such an inner-driven philosophy. But let me tell you a secret. The happiest wealthy people I know don't invest for diversification; they invest to keep their passion alive. How about you?

THE ANTIVENOM

At this point, you understand risk better than much of Wall Street does. What can be done to better your chances against it? Play with a pre-measured hand. While you can't win a game you don't play, you can't lose it either. The more you have to lose, the less aggressively you should play. Remember, risk has a shrewd personality. It is clandestine, and rarely shows its hand until it's too late for you. The wealthy person has no reason to have more chips on the table than he can lose.

While you can never fully insulate yourself against all possible risks, a better understanding of them can provide a "surprise buffer" —an umbrella of sorts. Life, unfortunately, has a lot more to do with what we don't know than what we do. Ask portfolio managers for their definition of risk. They will likely begin detailing a long list of vague terms. They have no better chance at understanding tomorrow than the palm reader in that $500 trailer. If one thing is for sure, it is that we should beware of that which seems absolutely certain.

Financial planning is guessing. Don't think so? Just pull out a financial plan written for you five years ago. How much of it came true? They're only guesses. I know it sounds frightening, but which is better—blindly following a projection when reality dictates a different path or adjusting to the new path as better information dictates? As a wealthy client, you don't need flattery, you need honesty, and here it is: Life is a journey traveled at night. Our prior experiences say the road is safe; after all, we've traveled the route a thousand times before. We engage our daily path with confidence. But our headlights only illuminate 200 feet in front of us; beyond this is complete darkness. We cannot see the pothole that wasn't there yesterday or the deer preparing to dart in front of our car. All we really know is what we see right now. Everything else is risk.

CHAPTER 4

The Financial Factory, Emotional Misdirection, and Other Tools of the Trade

The financial factory imprisons conversations on investing by leveraging inaccurate terms, namely, fear and greed. Fear and greed both reside at the far ends of our psychological compass. Yet, the financial factory wants you to believe this is our daily MO. It is not. Far more common is the emotional middle ground. This middle ground represents our desire for safety, security, self-preservation, and hope. But when motives have been misapplied at the beginning of any discussion, it is hard to perceive anything but extremes from that point forward.

Context is definition. How and where defines the what. You must take the time to define what is of value to you. Otherwise, anybody can change your context and thereby change your perspective.

It was as cold as it was early on January 12, 2007, when music began to populate the air. Not just any air, but the air of the L'Enfant Plaza in Washington, D.C. A man in his late thirties was playing a violin for any spare change he could attract. Hundreds of pedestrians raced by him without even a passing acknowledgment. After all, they had jobs; he didn't. They were on their way to important meetings with even more important people. He was basically a subway musician.

It seems no one took time to notice the complexity of the material. The man wasn't playing "Chopsticks" but, rather, classical masterpieces. Works like the Chaconne from Johann Sebastian Bach's Partita No. 2 in D Minor and Max Bruch's Violin Concerto in G Minor, both unfriendly to the untrained. Still, no one noticed. The pathos rising from his instrument should have arrested anyone who's ever been witness to unusual talent. Like seeing a thirteen-year-old pitch a 105-mile-per-hour fastball, some things should get your attention.

He wasn't playing just any violin, either; he was playing one of the best violins known to man: a Gibson ex-Huberman handcrafted by Antonio Stradivari himself in 1713. Its worth? $3.5 million. The sound was genius, his performance impeccable.

But the context was all wrong. Lottery-ticket kiosks, shoeshine stands, and the noise of unnecessary cell-phone conversations can dilute most anything of value. Still he played. After forty-five minutes, the open violin box had a grand total of $32. Never did a crowd gather, and only briefly did a few people stop to give ear to what they thought was possibly decent talent for a street musician. If they only had known.

It would be many months before news reports trickled out. Readers were shocked to learn what really happened that day. On the morning of January 12, more than a thousand people passed by one of the greatest violinists on earth. His name is Joshua Bell.

The idea for this experiment was birthed over coffee during the holidays. A fellow musician asked Bell if he'd be willing to put on street clothes and play in the middle of rush hour. The idea went from a joke to a consideration to a plan. On that winter's day, Bell—the world-renowned violinist who "plays like a god" according to Oscar-winning composer John Corigliano—was considered a mere mortal.

Without a tux, million-dollar acoustics, and an eighty-piece orchestra behind him, Bell was perceived differently by the crowd. His talent didn't change, but the context temporarily reduced his perceived value. Once your context changes, your perspective is soon to follow. If the most important thing to you is moving to Maui to write your memoir, then guess what will happen when an advisor says you should jump on the latest investment bandwagon? You'll recognize this suggestion as entanglement, not opportunity. Just as Joshua Bell learned, the environment doesn't change who you are, and neither should the market.

EXPERTISE CAN BE BLINDING

Price is brand. Forget logos, brochures, websites, and GEICO commercials. These are all secondary. Our money and how we arrive at a decision to separate ourselves from it is profoundly indicative. It not only says what we value but also why we value it. Branding at its fundamental level is the emotional connection we have to a product or service.

Consider this: When we pay for something expensive, we

experience an epinephrine-like high, although we may never consciously acknowledge this fact. It says first, "I can afford this." Second, the person selling the item or service knows I can afford it. We like this. It nurtures the very core of the human desire to accept and be accepted. So how does it work when something is cheap? It works the same way except on a different trajectory. Patronizing low prices feeds into our intellect. It says, "I'm smart."

No industry is more shrouded in subjective value and price than the wine industry. Open up a conversation about the best red wine and be prepared to stick around for a while. Wine enthusiasts are passionate, to put it mildly. And then you have the wine experts who think more highly of themselves than they ought. The wine expert can look at a bottle of pinot grigio and tell you not only the name of the field hand who picked the grape but the name of his second child too. They are fanatic.

Fanaticism does violence to context. Why does a bottle of 1992 Screaming Eagle cost $80,000? Why does a jeroboam of 1945 Chateau Mouton Rothschild cost $114,000? Because wine experts say that's what it's worth. They create the context; they define the value. It's that simple. The average bottle of wine pours six servings of four ounces each. For the Screaming Eagle, you're paying $13,000 per glass, and $19,000 per glass for the Mouton Rothschild. It's easy to see why wine enthusiasts would feel incredible accomplishment to own one of these wines. But what if the bottle of Screaming Eagle had been replaced with a $19.95 impostor? Of course it's impossible to fool wine experts, right? They smell better than bears and can taste "cheap" a mile away.

Not really.

Brain researchers in Europe asked the same question. To retrieve the answer, they traveled to the University of Bordeaux, the pinnacle of the wine-tasting world, and presented an interesting test. Wine aficionados regard white wines and red wines as completely different entities to be described in completely different ways. One is the sun; one is the moon. The researchers took bottles of white wine and inserted drops of odorless, tasteless red dye.[3] They gave the wine to the university wine experts, and the results were very revealing.

The experts were fooled. All accepted the wines as reds and quickly adhered to the accepted lexicon to explain their smell and tastes. Scientific authors Jay A. Gottfried and Raymond J. Dolan explained the results this way: "Human olfactory perception is notoriously unreliable, but shows substantial benefits from visual cues, suggesting important crossmodal integration between these primary sensory modalities."[4] In other words, we believe what we think we see.

Visual perception doesn't just assist in our perception; it defines it. Neither Joshua Bell nor the wine experts had a chance. The stern reality is that no matter how smart, educated, or talented a person may be, we can all be fooled—especially when we lose sight of context.

THE INVESTING STAGE

When the context for investing is relegated to extremes, one can never uncover, define, and deal with true motives. Ambition can be easily mislabeled as greed. Self-preservation and the desire for security are easily mislabeled as fear. I know a few greedy people, but none who operates in absolute greed every day without ceasing (you

---

3 http://www.cell.com/neuron/retrieve/pii/S0896627303003921.
4 Ibid. See also "Blind Tasting" at http://en.wikipedia.org/wiki/wine_tasting.

may know greedier people than I do). I know a few fearful ones too, but none who runs around hiding all day from an invisible enemy. To rely on the concepts of greed and fear is the most irresponsible act of emotional misdirection. Like an elegant virus, misdirection once released into public discourse is almost impossible to contain, much less cure. Using this narrative tool, the financial factory has manipulated the terms of the investment debate so that no matter who wins, you've won the wrong argument.

Why would the financial factory so violently skew the conversation? Because it is enormously profitable. The result is the creation of products designed to appeal to emotions.

THE SCRIPT

Have you noticed that most financial advisors say the same catch-phrases, read the same books, and recommend the same financial products? How can the same prescription be right for every person? What if I'm allergic to penicillin? No one even asks. The financial factory assumes all clients are the same. All need insurance, all clients must save, everyone needs stocks, and inflation is the boogeyman. The factory produces twenty-year retirement forecasts, and at the bottom of the same page, it makes a huge confession (they call it a disclaimer): PAST PERFORMANCE CANNOT BE USED TO PREDICT FUTURE RESULTS. It seems oddly hypocritical to produce a forecast for your life twenty years from now on the left side of the page, only to advise you not to rely on this projection on the opposite side. But this is the contradictory approach taught to the army of drones coming out of the financial factory.

For the record, I believe the CERTIFIED FINANCIAL PLANNER™ certification is important. It shows a commitment to the craft. Unfortunately, anybody can call him- or herself a financial planner, regardless of training or experience. Insurance agents, stockbrokers, and many financial advisors use the term *financial planner* to establish credibility to sell. The average financial plan is more of a fact-finding mission than a helpful map. It reveals exactly where to aim products—a raw sales process disguised as thoughtful assistance.

Granted, your financial advisor must be educated in the discipline of money management, but great advice only starts there. You can only give great advice once life has first advised you. Once turmoil and trauma have paid you a visit, you are better qualified to plan for your clients' futures. If you're going to teach a class on survival in a foxhole, it would be wise to have been in one yourself. Just as great investors possess invaluable advice for the new investor, great financial advisors have to have lived a little.

You cannot teach life experience in the factory. But life experience is the one irreplaceable ingredient all great advisors must have in their arsenal. It cannot be taught; it must be lived. This is why medical students don't practice on paper cutouts. They must touch and feel real skin, know the texture and shape of real organs, and smell the odors of the human body. They do this because in the hospital the stakes are much higher, the people are alive, and the families have placed the ultimate trust in their hands. The responsibilities placed in the hands of your advisor are very similar. You are asking that person to protect your way of life.

DRONES IN THE FACTORY

The factory permeates every brokerage firm, academic institution, financial product offering, financial media, and lobbyist, and the entire 401(k) investment complex, as well as Wall Street itself. The factory has a perspective. This perspective seeks to push you into a quantitative existence rather than a qualitative one. This means no matter how much money you have, you must get more. When quantity controls your decisions, you over-invest and therefore over-risk. The factory force fits you into a position made for the aspirational rich, those who are seeking what you already have. The aspirational rich are constantly looking for the next great investment idea. Unfortunately, many wealthy persons do the same thing. And therein lies the disconnection. No one tells the wealthy clients they can stop desperately looking for the "next thing." No one tells them they've already won.

This question always comes as a surprise to clients sitting in front of me, so now let me ask you: Did you know you are a winner? The game is over. You won. At this point, you don't need to invest for profit; you need to allocate your wealth in a way that sustains your lifestyle, forever. Whether you know it or not, you are at a cross-roads. Crossroads are a great analogy because they force a decision. Both paths cannot be engaged simultaneously. Either go left or go right—or stay still. When you have money, everything you read in the financial pornography section of your local bookstore encourages you to take one path. This path is called over-investing.

What is dangerous about choosing the path of over-investing is it assumes you need more. It assumes you don't have enough. It assumes you haven't won. Winners don't run past the finish line; if they did, the crowd would surely yell, "Stop! You've already won the race!" This accurately represents the disconnectedness of the financial services industry to the wealthy client. Wealthy clients have different options, and they need to speak to professionals who understand these options.

For example, when you sit in front of a quantitatively driven financial advisor, he doesn't value your love of art. He doesn't understand the passion you have for one day opening your own gallery to highlight the fifty paintings you've done over the last twenty years. He doesn't get it, because that is a qualitative existence. Better yet, maybe you have always wanted to take guitar lessons, record a CD, and travel the world playing your songs. Whether your dream is creative, charitable, or recreational, you are the keeper of your happiness.

The quantitative model seeks to keep you concentrated solely on the numbers. The qualitative model seeks to keep you concentrated on your happiness and designs a financial model around this core objective.

Too often I meet with wealthy couples suffering from toxic advice. All they needed was a different investment perspective, one that focuses on maintaining wealth, not creating it from scratch. If they understood their Point of Independence (which we will discuss later), they would have risked little while maintaining much. Instead, they kept playing, and it cost them more than it paid.

When you perpetually invest, you become oblivious to your status as a winner; you concentrate less on the things that make you happy. Your dreams are delayed. You must know when you've crossed the finish line.

A VIEW FROM THE INSIDE

"The rogue broker has now become the rogue brokerage firm." I heard these words in a meeting with Pat Sadler, an Atlanta-based securities attorney. Sadler has more than twenty-five years' experience representing investors who have been bludgeoned by the factory.

"Most people don't understand that the only purpose of their account is to generate income so the firm can meet its monthly expenses," Sadler said. He went on to explain why risk questionnaires and conversations on risk tolerance and volatility are designed to reduce the legal liability of the firm. The one-size-fits-all approach goes into immediate action the moment you wire money into your account. The traditional financial firm is going to manage your money exactly like they manage everyone else's. Regardless of what they may tell you, there is no consideration of your specific situation. For the wealthy client, the difference is on the front end. The difference is the sales process and the financial resources that a firm is willing to commit in order to make you a client.

This became crystal clear when I was fortunate enough to interview a former Internet executive; we'll call him Thomas. Thomas became enormously wealthy through the creation and sale of an international company. His insights should be a required class in Staying Wealthy 101.

So I asked Thomas to start at the beginning. First, I wanted to know how private equity and wealth management firms found him. After all, he wasn't wealthy to begin with. He had no history of family wealth or Wall Street relationships. He explained how, the moment he and his business partners began to float the very idea of selling, the phone began to ring. Not only did the phone ring; the people on the other end knew how much he stood to gain, and when he stood to gain it. This points to an incestuous relationship among bankers, private equity, underwriters, and private wealth divisions. If you're about to become wealthy, you'll show up on the financial factory radar like an L-1011 approaching the White House.

Again, all of this potential wealth had yet to materialize. Oh, did I mention the factory does its homework? Thomas loves golf. Can you imagine what happened next? A private wealth manager invited him on a golf outing, a foursome. Somehow, one of the players in the foursome was Fred Couples. This is an ingenious psychological move. It is chess at the Bobby Fischer level.

The factory establishes shared experiences based on your passions. This promotes a sense of reciprocity. Think about it; would he ever have been able to play a round with Fred Couples? Of course not. Such a fond memory knits a relationship to the private wealth manager even though in reality no relationship exists. A person having experienced such a momentous event with such a legend would feel more comfortable turning over millions to the agent who brokered his happiness. It is absolutely brilliant.

The golf event was followed with an offer to travel to New York for an all-expense-paid weekend in which Thomas and his wife would be treated as royalty. The catch is, there's just one more meeting.

THE MEETING

Thomas sat at a table with a group of polished professionals. The introductions began something like this. "First, we want to tell you how honored we are to be in your presence. You've become wealthy at a very young age, which places you in the rarest of company. Congratulations is an understatement."

They continued. "We want you to meet our team. Kathy here is our most seasoned estate planner. She has seen everything. She has served our wealthy client base with invaluable insight over many years. At this stage, your questions will be different. She is available to answer them all." The introductions went straight down the line from financial planning professionals to investment "experts." Then, as if to counter any amateurish objections, the conversation took a slight turn.

Thomas said the lead wealth manager began to make several assertions. First, he commented on how many individuals who are new to wealth don't understand the challenges of growing and keeping it. Second, he said the talents that made you wealthy won't keep you wealthy; you need people who specialize. Third, he told Thomas that a few people sat right where he was sitting and refused their services, and that these people suffered. Thomas decided to take his chances and be one of those who refused. In his mind, he made his wealth investing in companies, so that's what he would continue doing. It was uncomfortable to say no in the face of overwhelming professionalism, intelligence, and confidence. After all, these people are really nice. But in a slaughterhouse, even the vegetarians have blood on their hands. He decided to dance with the girl he brought. He remains wealthy.

SMILEY FACES

When you have money, there are smiling faces everywhere. *Eccentric* replaces *confused*, and ideas previously considered crazy are labeled ingenious. When you have money, your bank offers services not printed in their brochures. Car dealers shed tears of joy when you pull up to the lot, and financial advisors never utter that four-letter curse word: "Stop."

YOU SHOULD ONLY HAVE TO GET RICH ONCE

Money does more than talk; it sings the most beautiful of melodies. Everyone knows the money song and wants to sing along. This is because our society is based on insatiable consumption. Consumption never gives; it only takes. But it takes away so gradually one can easily forget its true danger.

Think of consumption as a twenty-four-hour concierge desk covering the width and breadth of the earth. It is exquisitely appointed with the best personal services available anywhere. This desk has only one customer policy—to give you whatever you want, whenever you want it, for a price.

It's no mystery why people with resources are treated differently. This wouldn't be a bad thing if it didn't concurrently birth so many complexities. Money makes it very difficult to hear the truth. Everything is tweaked for positive consumption in an effort to "keep the money happy." It is a cruel trap, because the same financial resources that open so many doors of commerce close so many doors of common sense.

ENABLERS

When you have money, honesty is an endangered species. And one group is especially notorious for making us feel good about our bad decisions. Some people call them yes-men, but most know them as enablers. Enablers are everywhere. In our context, their only purpose is to help the wealthy delay facing the negative consequences of ill-advised decisions. Ironically, avoiding these negative consequences only intensifies the pain when truth must finally be faced.

Certain enablers keep you running so long that you forget the concept of finishing the race. The most dangerous enablers personally believe the story they're telling you. The stories are always great. The more you hear, the better it sounds. You then begin to insert yourself into the story and transfer the triumphs to yourself. You start to see potential. There's only one problem—you are already successful, already triumphant. You've already won, but the enabler convinces you there is still more sweetness to be enjoyed, which is like telling you to chew yesterday's gum.

Some enablers are pseudo-psychologists; they understand persuasion and human behavior like few others. Great enablers can finish your sentences. They get you the second drink before the first one is started. They possess an acute skill of managing your vices in advance. If you believe you must always be in the market, a financial enabler will find a way to keep you invested, forever.

Anyone who has ever gone to Alcoholics Anonymous understands the enabler profile all too well. Enablers put a positive twist on the worst of habits, saying it was only one drink too many or calling the drunk driving charge a temporary lapse in judgment. Even in the face of overwhelming evidence, enablers find an out for you, a better excuse, or an ingenious cover-up. Enablers uproot the stop signs at every intersection only to blame the crash on someone else. And even though one may have little contact with enablers, they seem to show up at the perfectly wrong time. Their input is potent. It has been said that 90 percent of rat poison is harmless household cornstarch; it's the remaining 10 percent, the strychnine, that does the killing. Enablers can be like strychnine.

For the wealthy, traditional financial advisors flirt with the enabler profile. Now this may sound a bit harsh, so let me place my critique in proper context. Business schools, brokerage houses, and financial planning programs all indoctrinate their students with a nearly impenetrable philosophy that says, "You must maximize your resources to be happy." It is a factory, and factories produce the same products all day, every day, without modification.

Financial products don't do the right things as much as they make us feel the right way. Millions of us wear old shoes, drive archaic vehicles, and refuse to throw away that thirty-year-old sweater because of one thing: It makes us feel good. New financial products are designed to do just this; they make us feel warm and cared for. We like knowing we bought into a new fund. We like getting in on the ground floor. We like feeling smart. A new financial product is no different from an iPhone. Everyone has one, and we will not be left out.

MACY'S PARADE

I can empathize with most financial professionals because financial programs create advisors who are more like Macy's mannequins. We don't blame the mannequins in the window for being inflexible; they were designed to be that way. They only wear the clothes put on them; they promote the fashions given to them. They have no choice but to toe the party line. So now imagine a warm-blooded, moving and speaking mannequin with a finance degree, and you've just described the average financial advisor.

This type of financial advisor works for a time. Dave Ramsey, Clark Howard, and Suze Orman are perfect for the aspirational. Shows like *Fast Money*, Jim Cramer's *Mad Money*, and CNBC's *Squawk Box* keep the fiery dream of becoming rich burning bright. They aren't for you. The real issue is not whether traditional financial advice has anything good to offer; it is whether it has anything good for you, the wealthy client.

BING! BING! BONG!

The factory is so powerful because human nature seeks patterns, and the factory provides them. We seek repetition more than creativity. Ad agencies know this, so they spend millions on getting celebrities to endorse their products. And for every celebrity wearing a shirt, millions of customers will fall in line and wear it also. Advertisers start the pattern, and we finish it. But there's an even better example of how deeply rooted our desire for the comfort of patterns and repetition is.

The World Science Festival is an annual event bringing together the best scientific and creative minds of this generation. The magic of this conference is the width and breadth of its participants. The June 12, 2009, festival had a rather revealing theme: "Notes & Neurons: In Search of the Common Chorus." The overarching question posed during this segment was whether our response to music is hardwired or culturally determined, whether the human reaction to rhythm and melody is universal or influenced by our environment. But even further, how does the human mind respond to cues, especially cues we've never heard or seen before? And lastly, how does this construct carry to other areas of our lives as we seek to recognize and participate in systems with systematic philosophies? What they found was rather revealing.

To illustrate whether the human response to patterns was innate or culturally determined, guest artist and panelist Bobby McFerrin took the stage. McFerrin is an internationally respected jazz vocalist, but that term is limiting of his true ability. He combines music with an almost Lion King–like sensibility as he seems to be able to sing not only notes but also attitudes, characters, and nature itself.

McFerrin stands at center stage in front of a packed audience.

He begins to jump up and down in place. While jumping, he hums a note and motions the audience to join him in humming it. They do. He then jumps faster and faster and the audience in turn repeats the notes faster, matching his tempo. Then McFerrin, without warning, jumps two feet to his left and automatically the entire audience sings the next logical, higher note in total unison. For the next two minutes, McFerrin bounces around stage with the audience all assuming together what the next note should be. They sing it on time and without variance. Once McFerrin taught the first two notes, he didn't have to teach any more. An audience of hundreds correctly filled in the blanks.[5] How is this?

Behavioral finance studies the social, cognitive, and emotional factors involved in economic decisions. The theory that best describes how McFerrin's cognitive example affects our financial decisions is called herd behavior. As you can infer by the name, "herd behavior" describes how individuals can act together in unison without planning. All it requires is an observable act to get the ball rolling, and the masses will perfectly fill in the blanks. Our desire to belong and not be left out is many times stronger than our desire to express our individual voice.

Imagine what would have happened had thirty individuals out of the audience of thousands decided to sing a different note. What if they decided to ascribe a different intonation to McFerrin's movements? Would they have been wrong? No. Would they have been negatively noticed? Yes. Their notes would have caused dissonance and seemed out of place when, in reality, they would have simply been expressing their personal "passion," if you will. It takes confidence to

---

5   http://www.youtube.com/watch?v=ne6tB2KiZuk.

be different, but some of the best results grow out of unique actions made by people not afraid to sing a different tune.

EXECUTIVE BOATING

A very good friend told me an interesting story of an IBM executive and a boat guide. Guess which one retired at forty-two? In an effort to find inspiration and motivation, the IBM executive coughed up $7,000 to travel down the Colorado River with a large group. The executive was exhausted on many levels and searching to break the dangerous tunnel vision caused by his daily routine—the tunnel vision that says, "Get a good education and a good job, work hard, make money, save, and retire too late to enjoy any of it." He had two mortgages, kids in private school, and a spouse spending his money like there was no tomorrow. After a few days on the Colorado, the boat guide, who was getting paid to charter the trip of a lifetime, became frustrated listening to the executive whine about his privileged, pitiful life. So he tells the executive in a short but respectful way, "You know, I have been retired since I was forty-two." This statement surprised the executive so much he nearly fell out of the boat.

From a very young age the executive, along with millions of us, was taught to be compliant, do the work, make an A, and then move to the next level. This construct never prepares you for the realities of life, the stress, disappointments, and surprises no one tells you about. His problem was this: When he sat down to plan this thirty-year trip called "career," he planned it using an outdated map. This map didn't show him it was okay to forge a different path. It didn't display which roads were rerouted due to structural changes or how quickly his climbing age would erode his value and opportunities in the marketplace. The map couldn't show this.

Consequently, he was shocked when his actual career had little to no resemblance to the trip he planned years earlier. Sickness, accidents, and potholes are never seen on a map. Maps represent how things were, not how they will be tomorrow. The executive thought two homes, four cars, and expensive toys would make him happy. He wasn't. And now he was paying $7,000 to find inspiration drifting down the Colorado River. Ironically, although the driver of the boat was making a peasant's sum to guide the trip, he understood more about living than did his wealthy passenger. He understood simplicity; he understood the value of quality time.

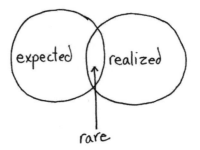

I have one friend who is an ex-pilot turned financial planner, and another who is a doctor turned planner. I actually believe these individuals are better than those advisors who originate from the factory. They see things differently, and that is probably the most important skill of a good planner. You cannot properly learn this business in school. Learning how to correctly advise doesn't come from financial programs. These programs will teach you about Monte Carlo, retirement planning, how bonds and equities work, basic taxation, insurance products, and more. They will teach you how the machine works, but you won't learn when not to use the machine or how to discern when the machine itself is flawed.

Traditional financial advisors make money when you stick to the script and buy their products. It is much easier to scare you into investing than inspire you to go live your life and follow your passions.

20/20

This book is a pair of reading glasses. The industry will not change, but how you view it will. Your vision will be sharper, your contrast more definite. The context from which every piece of investment advice emerges will be clearer. Motives will surface. In other words, you won't pass Joshua Bell in the Metro station again. You'll notice what no one else does.

While your financial goal line will seem to appear out of nowhere, let me assure you, it's been there the entire time. Only now you'll be able to see it.

CHAPTER 5

Financial Drug Dealers & Mansions on the Moon

Their similarities force my hand into comparison. I refer to the current financial planning model and illegal drug dealers. Both must have product, great salesmanship, and an efficient distribution system. Both push an exciting future based on temporary highs.

Illegal drug dealers leverage elements of human nature. First, they create a product that overrides logic. Second, it's readily available everywhere, all the time. Third, they market, market, market. Dealers understand people will chase the original high for decades. They will never find it but will look forever.

Did you know that most financial firms operate on a similar premise? They use more sophisticated packaging, and of course they don't stand on street corners—yet. Financial firms peddle a drug called profit.

A HEROIN-LIKE HIT

Profit can be an addictive narcotic. Everyone wants it. People will do anything to get a hit of it in their portfolio. It's such a rush when a stock you bought for $30 is now trading at $60. You feel smart; you feel like you were right. You begin to weave your own favorable context. If you're wondering how powerful context is, please turn back and read chapter 4.

Once they get a hit of profit, investors, like addicts, seek the next best thing; whether they need money is irrelevant. No one tells them that, once you have money, it's all about risk of return, not rate of return.

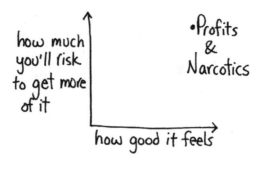

THE PATH TOWARD ADDICTION

We encountered a major challenge to traditional financial planning in the late 1990s. This is when a universal standard of 10 percent became known as equity rate of return. The concept was to invest in equity and get 10 percent every single year. But the variance of the 10 percent became more important than the 10 percent itself. During the tech boom, expectation of market returns got out of hand. The computer age arrived along with financial planning software. Programs like Efficient Frontier and Monte Carlo permeated the industry, providing a false sense of security. One could run hypothetical investments to discern the "best" portfolio makeup. It was magic. It was addictive. It was a drug.

Many of these software programs put 100 percent of assets in some type of emerging market's small-cap fund. It was pretty clear the new frontier was garbage. At the time, academics shrugged their shoulders as if this type of allocation were just an acceptable side effect, advising us to change the assumptions to get the result we wanted. Very scary.

REALITY SETTLES IN

Then came the bust of 2000, which meant investors who relied on a 10 percent return to continue their lifestyle hit rock bottom. They failed because they were deceived into making permanent plans based on variable returns.

Somehow, wealthy clients have been convinced they need profit like everyone else. In this context, financial advisors and stockbrokers are street suppliers of choice. They have the good stuff—the best software, the best research, and the best projections.

TOOLS OF THE TRADE

Financial drug dealers design investment projections like a realtor selling mansions on the moon. The story feels so good you begin to believe it's attainable. Stories are always kept at the highest level, where logic can't reach. After all, who wants to answer questions like "Where will I shop on the moon?" or "Where will the kids go to school up there?"

You may have heard it put this way: "We care about your goals. We'll help you realize your dreams, and we will invest your money in an intelligent way to achieve your objectives . . ." Sounds great, doesn't it?

Moreover, the advisor—let's say it's a man, but it certainly needn't be—usually believes the story he's telling you. The dealer will then pull out pretty graphs and charts. He'll show you attractive market returns too good to turn down.

Chances are you'll then hear a narrative about one of his clients who made a fortune following his advice. All of this implies the same thing can happen to you. Everything is packaged to get another addict. You'll hear little about the side effects of this drug called profit. Side effects like losses are all covered under a heading like, "Past Performance Is Not Indicative of Future Results."

The factory is constantly working to create new products. The new ones will be equally polished and promise great results with limited risk. Recently, the worst offenders have included:

- Hedge funds
- Insurance contracts packaged as investments
- Structured notes
- Auction-rate securities

Hedge Funds

This is a hard one to grasp, but anytime somebody takes a product available to everyone and puts their logo on it, they are taking generic bleach and making it expensive bleach. The worst example of "expensive bleach" is hedge funds. Most hedge funds buy the same securities you can buy. But because hedge fund managers claim to be smarter, they should get paid more. Right?

"Giving incentives to teach well is like giving a bonus to a fish for swimming—it's simply inappropriate," said Katie L. Challen, a private school teacher in Alpharetta, Georgia. Schoolteachers who fudge student performance numbers and hedge fund managers may seem like an odd comparison. But once you study the psychological similarities one thing becomes clear: Performance incentives may have dangerous side effects.

A hedge fund is not an asset class; it is a compensation structure. The black box you throw your money into is designed to reward outstanding performance. Your money can be invested in almost anything. The baseline compensation of the manager is usually 1.5 percent per year, and if the fund meets its annual performance objectives the manager is entitled to 20 percent of the additional profits. On the surface, it seems like common sense that you'll get better results if you provide a monetary incentive. Anyone who excels at school, on the football field, at work, or at managing money should get a bonus. And the larger the bonus, the more motivation to excel.

For a hedge fund manager to excel, he has to be creative. He has to see things other people don't see, capture opportunities before the world wakes up, or implement strategies that make money when no one else is making money. He has to not just be good but really good. According to an article titled "The Index Funds Win Again," published in the *New York Times* on February 22, 2009, the average hedge fund would need to earn 19 percent before taxes, fees, and expenses to surpass the performance of an index fund making 10 percent. Even ignoring the reality that finding someone like that is next to impossible, the monetary incentive to perform may be toxic to your wealth.

In their book *Freakanomics*, authors Steven D. Levitt and Stephen J. Dubner discuss the unintended consequences of the No Child Left Behind Act. In 1996, the Chicago Public School System implemented high-stakes performance incentives. Teachers would now be held accountable for their poorly performing students. In addition, the school system stopped progressing students if they did not make the minimum score on the Iowa Test of Basic Skills. Teachers had a big incentive for their kids to perform. What did some teachers do? They cheated. Levitt created an algorithm to detect questionable test results. Looking at more than 100 million test questions from 1993 to 2000, which bracketed the introduction of incentives, a noticeable spike in test scores occurred in 1996. The cheating algorithm organized the data by classroom and by teacher. The Chicago public school system took the results seriously and retested the classrooms suspected of cheating against a control group of classrooms. The retest took place several weeks later, and as the algorithm had predicted, the teachers suspected of cheating on student test scores dropped dramatically. Less than a decade later, the Atlanta public school system repeated history with its own Southern version of the Chicago cheating scandal.

Daniel Pink, in his book *Drive*, discusses the unintended consequences of incentives. We exercise because we want to, we help others because it feels good, and we play Scrabble because it's fun. But what happens if you pay someone to do something that should be fun? It becomes work. Children who get paid to solve puzzles solve them more slowly than kids who do it for free. Children who are paid to read three books rarely pick up a fourth. Salespeople who hit their sales target for the quarter go home. Corporate executives massage their quarterly earnings to meet earnings estimates. And the Wall Street performance-bonus structure nearly bankrupted not just America but also the global economy. Money can be a very bad influence when attached to a goal.

Why is this? Goals create tunnel vision; goals narrow the focus on the predetermined result. The goal increases the likelihood of risks; it increases the likelihood of unethical behavior, and creates selfishness. Goals are addictive, like a sugar rush in our brain. All of this leads to short-term thinking, which can lead to bad choices and very bad results.

If you want your money manager to worry about you, pay him a fair wage. If you want him to worry about himself, pay him a performance fee.

My natural bias against hedge funds is based on seeing too many people disappointed by their lofty promises.

Insurance Contracts Packaged as Investments

Whenever I encounter an irreparable situation, insurance "investment" products are usually accessories to the crime. Often, they are the prime suspect. These products come in various shapes and sizes but are all equally toxic to your independence.

Whole life, universal life, variable universal life, variable annuities, and indexed annuities are the current names, but marketing departments coin new ones all the time to hide history.

These products taunt our intelligence. To market them one must use terms that cannot logically coexist. Growing assets and maintaining absolute safety are mutually exclusive. They don't mix.

My cranberry muffin breakfast was destroyed one morning as I overheard an advisor selling an indexed annuity to a hopeful investor one table over. He used more word combinations than Sesame Street. One particular word stuck with me. He said, "Investing in this product will increase your *growability*." Is that a word? It sure sounds good. And that's the problem with these presentations. They are designed to make us feel good about doing a very bad thing.

If you remember nothing else from this book, remember this: NEVER BUY AN INSURANCE PRODUCT FOR INVESTMENT PURPOSES.

After reading a draft of this book, my friend Tim asked me to help him understand an insurance product. If it worked, the product would achieve every goal he ever desired. Income for life, guaranteed rate of return, and growth of principal would all be his. He was excited! Fortunately, Tim is a lawyer and well aware of one fact: The big print giveth and the small print taketh away.

He was certain this product had a trap door but damned if he could figure it out. Tim, like many people with money, had suffered from bad investment experience with a series of advisors. Over the previous ten years, his net worth hadn't changed at all, so he began searching for something different.

Tim spoke with friends about his frustration, and magically a financial planner (really an insurance agent in disguise) delivered a product to solve all his problems. I stopped by his office and picked up the brochure. It was a marketing masterpiece.

Scattered throughout the glossy brochure are emotional buzzwords like *build, guarantee, protect*. Pretty charts and graphs show you how rich you'll become while never risking a penny of principal. Nonchalantly placed in the package is an informational CD.

I popped it in and a 330-plus-page rulebook populated my screen. Who would read this stuff? (Me—I need a life.)

Buried in these pages was the cost of ownership. I don't want to bore you with all the details, so here is my Cliff's Notes version:

- Financial advisor (insurance agent in disguise) says $1,000,000 investment will allow Tim to grow his money while guaranteeing principal.

- Tim will have to keep this contract ten years to avoid the surrender penalty.

- Maximum cost of ownership over ten years, assuming a 5 percent rate of return: $727,000.

- Maximum cost of ownership over ten years, assuming a 5 percent rate of return: $727,000 (in case you missed it the first time).

For comparison purposes, I pulled up the Vanguard Index 500 (VFINX) mutual fund prospectus; the same $1,000,000 investment is projected to cost $23,000 over ten years.[6] Ignoring the over-investing problem and other issues I have with the Index 500 fund, Tim could lose $700,000 in the stock market and still be better off!

When confronted with these facts, the corporate headquarters tried their best to help him "understand" it better. Without hesitation, the agent stated, "It is the most expensive product we sell and it's not for everyone, only those willing to commit to their future." Masterful. Caught, confessed, and still selling. You can't make this stuff up.

Tim stood his ground, fought the factory, and won.

---

6 https://personal.vanguard.com/us/LiteratureRequest?FW_Activity=ViewOnlineActivity&litID=22100 51310&FW_Event=start&cbdForceDomain=false.

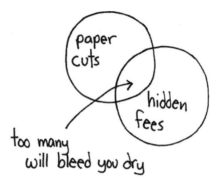

too many
will bleed you dry

In another encounter, I watched as a financial advisor (another insurance agent in disguise) built the most glorious illustration for me. He showed me how to use life insurance to grow tax-free retirement income for clients. I've seen this presentation many times but figured I'd sharpen my teeth. We sat down for lunch and the conversation went a little like this:

> **Agent:** Using this product, Brenda will be able to fund her retirement tax-free and receive a $3.5 million insurance policy on her life. (He slides the presentation over to my side of the table.)

> **Me:** Let me get this straight. You want Brenda to write a check for $75,000 for the next fifteen years to fully fund an insurance policy on her life? And then at age sixty-five, you show her getting $100,000 per year tax-free for the next twenty years?

> **Agent:** Yes, and while the "Guaranteed" column[7] does not show this happening, our company has always paid a dividend higher than the guarantees.

---

7   Guaranteed column represents a list of accumulated values that are good as long as the issuing company doesn't go bankrupt.

Me: Great! So let me work this through out loud so I understand. You want Brenda to write checks totaling $1,125,000 over the next fifteen years?

Agent: Yes, but you would only buy this with surplus investment capital that she wants to grow tax-free.

Me: And if she changes her mind or something happens in her life in the next ten years and she had to get her money back, it shows here that she would lose money on the policy?

Agent: Yes.

Me: And the only way she can get her money at retirement is to take a loan against the cash value? Or die?

Agent: Well, we don't explain it that way but essentially yes.

Me: So why would anybody want to do this? It sounds more like a mortgage on a house. You work for fifteen years to pay it off and then turn around and remortgage the house at retirement and call it tax-free income. Seems sort of deceptive to me. What am I missing?

Agent: [Silence]

So what does all of this prove? It proves how dangerous insurance products sold as investments are to your wealth. It proves that if you're willing to lock up your capital for fifteen to twenty years, anybody can deliver on a promise. And if they don't, you have forgotten what the promise was anyway. It proves that products requiring Bible-length documentation hide the truth. It proves that insurance is not an investment.

Structured Notes

Structured notes represent financial engineering at its worst. Financial engineering takes simple products and creates complex derivatives within them to generate sales and commissions. The risks that result from such products cannot be clearly measured. They are as unnatural as crossbreeding a goat with a Chihuahua. Some things just shouldn't happen.

I originally intended not to discuss structured notes. I thought the wooden dagger had been pressed securely into this category's heart, the dagger being a combination of clients who lost tons of money investing in them and books about Wall Street misconduct. My favorite book on the subject is Frank Partnoy's *Infectious Greed: How Deceit and Risk Corrupted the Financial Markets,* in which he details the beginnings of the structured note.

Partnoy discusses the first version of these products, which came to market in the late 1980s. He delves deep into the toxic nature of derivatives. He shows how new financial products were created to be complex—so clients could not understand them—and to generate huge fees selling them.

Structured notes blossomed from their inception to the mid-1990s. The purpose was to get clients invested in equities to generate fees, but this product also created an illusion of security when Wall Street called it a bond. The outcome for investors was not good.

I decided to include structured notes in this book because one of my clients forwarded me a "Structured Products Strategies Guide". The broker who sent my client the guide stated, "One of these is a 5 year Certificate of Deposit (FDIC insured) whose return is linked to the performance of a basket of 10 stocks including Chevron, 3M, Kraft, GE, McDonalds, and Coke." The broker goes on to say, "This might be a way for those hesitant about getting back into stocks to gain some equity exposure." I've summarized the terms of the offering below so you can follow along. Please pardon me if it's rather pedantic. I'm not sure I understand it.

The bank is FDIC insured and the interest is linked to ten underlying shares (3M, Aetna, AT&T, Boston Scientific, Chevron, Coca-Cola, GE, Kraft, McDonald's, Newmont Mining). The CD matures in five years and offers 100 percent protection with only two footnotes. Footnote number one: Payments are subject to the creditworthiness of the bank. Any element of protection is available only if the product is held to maturity and is subject to the creditworthiness of the issuer. (Are you lost yet?) Footnote number two: In the event the issuer fails, only the principal amount of the product is protected by the FDIC and only up to statutory limits. The maximum interest rate is 3.35 percent to 4.35 percent per period (which is defined as semiannually) and 6.70 percent to 8.70 percent per annum.

Following so far? Here's more explanation: The return cap/floor is 3.35 percent to 4.35% / - 15%. The variable interest rate for any semiannual period will be determined by averaging the returns of each underlying share from the trade date to the applicable semiannual observation date, with each underlying share return adjusted upward to the return floor of - 15 percent or adjusted downward to the return cap as applicable. The variable interest rate for any interest period will not be less than 0 percent.

Are you still there?

If you can figure out how much you will get paid, you're smarter than I am. So here's the challenge for you, the wealthy client. This product contains the illusion of certainty—FDIC insurance and ten well-known stocks. Even I felt it couldn't be that bad. After all, these are great companies. But here's the problem: This product has no market. Nobody will buy this from you because they can't figure out what it's worth, and neither can you. It's a mansion on the moon.

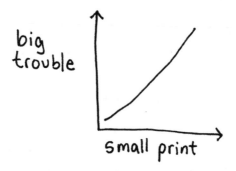

In Nassim Taleb's 2010 update of his 2007 bestseller, *The Black Swan: The Impact of the Highly Improbable*, he created ten principles for a "Black-Swan-robust" society. Number 6: "Do not give children dynamite sticks, even if they come with a warning label." Complex financial products need to be banned because nobody understands them, and few prospects are rational enough to know it. The factory knows we seek certainty, and it purposely creates products to encourage precisely that illusion.

The next product went extinct, but only after taking a lot of money from a lot of wealthy people. We are still living in its wake. Bad financial products are like too much radiation; the detrimental effects linger for a long time.

Auction-Rate Securities

In 1984, Ronald Gallatin of the now defunct Lehman Brothers created the auction-rate security. This bit of backroom alchemy didn't become famous until 2001, however. It's the latest example of insiders portraying trial and error as riskless investing. Liz Moyer, staff writer for Forbes.com, explained auction-rate securities this way in a May 2008 exposé[8] of the ill-conceived product: "There are bad

---

8   http://www.forbes.com/2008/05/08/auction-rate-bonds-biz-wall-cx_lm_0508auctionrate.html.

investments, and then there are really, really bad investments." The article went on to describe the product as "obscure and increasingly toxic."

In theory, auction-rate securities were supposed to act like cash. They allow issuers, municipalities, and student loan lenders to get preferred borrowing terms on long-term debt. Unfortunately, when the credit markets went haywire, the auctions began to fail, which means investors holding ARSs had nowhere to sell them. They were left holding a financial security with no liquidity. Which is kinda like owning a mansion on the moon—great location but no one can get to it.

Making this worse, ARSs reset at higher penalty rates if auctions fail, similar to adjustable-rate mortgages. Consequently, the ARSs issuers began to suffer.

In Moyer's May 2008 article, she revealed that $5 billion of auction-rate securities issued by Pennsylvania Higher Education Assistance Agency, one of the biggest in the market, were reset to zero. The investors in these securities include thousands of ordinary people who thought they were buying money-market securities, according to Karen Tyler, the state securities regulator in North Dakota and president of the North American Securities Administrators Association. Instead, these investors are stuck and can't sell without taking a loss. And according to Tyler, many have locked up funds originally set aside for mortgage down payments, living expenses, small-business payrolls, and, in the case of farmers, spring planting funds.

Twelve states and the SEC are investigating how investment banks marketed and sold auction-rate securities.

These banks sold ARSs like every other toxic financial product: with confidence. They were designed to provide safety but in the end were only mansions on the moon.

CHAPTER 6

Weeds Don't Need Fertilizer

If left alone, a yard will grow into disarray, not order. Understanding that life tends to lean away from our desired outcomes is the beginning of wisdom.

Anyone who has ever purchased stock or made a private investment knows one thing—the timing of negative events is inexplicable. Stocks rarely go up when you buy them, and the market always takes longer to correct itself when your money is on the line. It isn't personal, although it sure seems that way.

The market doesn't know your name. At play is the natural tendency for weeds to grow. Without pruning, watering, or care, weeds thrive. This fact became even more evident after seeing a recent advertisement.

VACATION RESORT IDEA GONE WRONG

The British accent was spot on. So were the cinematic pans of surrounding nature. Deer were running, flowers were blooming, and the intimate scenes of the spa were to die for. I was ready to buy my ticket. No doubt this new resort spent millions on the best minds in branding and marketing. I'm sure they were given a market analysis report second to none. Given the number of five-star resorts in the world, you would have to do no less to cut through the luxury vacation market. The commercial was ending, and as I reached for my credit card, the name was announced—Sandy Balls Resort.

Surely this must be a joke. Had I missed a hint of dry humor in the announcer voice? Was there evidence of a *Saturday Night Live*–type buildup in the story, music, or actors? Something was afoot, because no company would put millions into building a marketing campaign and then name a new resort after something found in a jock strap. It wasn't a joke. This is the name of the actual vacation resort. Take a minute to think about that.

And if you are still wondering, Google the name. It's a real place, a real business, a real bad marketing idea.

Like weeds, bad ideas are everywhere. Bad ideas grow in the midst of the greatest minds and circumvent the greatest strategies known to man. The best training, experience, analysis, and proofing is no match for the errant weed. Think about how many people looked at the words Sandy Balls before it was published to the world. The marketing agency, attorneys, CPAs, signage company, scriptwriters, website designers, and even the guy narrating the commercials all did. How many times do you think one or many of them said, "This is a horrific name!" What do you think kept them from voicing their concerns to the decision makers? And if they did voice their concerns, what do you think kept the powers that be on a path toward moniker failure?

For the hired hands, it could have been fear, neglect, or indifference. After all—it's not their money. The most dangerous weeds are those in plain sight but nevertheless ignored. By the time you figure out how deep the weeds have grown, your entire garden is choked.

THE NATURE OF NATURE

Quackgrass, bentgrass, chickweed, clover, crabgrass, dandelions, and ground ivy are just a small list of weeds growing in your lawn. Whether you are attentive or neglectful, weeds will find their way in. One reason weeds are so powerful is that they are not bound by territory. Weeds are mobile.

Weed seeds can be carried by wind or water for miles. In other words, your property can suffer from something not homegrown. A brisk wind can pick up weeds growing ten houses down from you and deposit them in your yard; you must now clean up someone else's mess. Sound familiar? We'll return to that point a little later.

THE COMMON THREAD

In many ways, horticulturalists understand bad events better than economists do. They understand that bad things just happen. The professional lawn care person spends no time growing weeds. Weeds don't need fertilizer.

There is a profound lesson here for the financial advisor and the investor alike. Despite all the time spent planning, filling out useless risk questionnaires, or studying the markets, bad financial events just show up.

I'm not a psychologist, but I do know that the behavior of the wealthy client is rapidly changing. The most recent market crash has removed much of the façade the financial industry depended on. Common sense is making a rebound, and people are questioning the "experts" like never before. It is critically important to remember one thing: If we considered all the things that can go wrong at every turn, we would be frozen in place. No one can function properly while concentrating on all the negative possibilities life has to offer. So the challenge is to plan for bad events without dwelling on them. The point is to enjoy the majesty of the ocean while wearing your life jacket.

A SOLID INVESTMENT

By 2000, Sarah B. had amassed a $10 million net worth. She was an early minority partner in a Silicon Valley microchip company. While meeting with her advisor, Sarah was presented with a solid, legitimate investment opportunity.

Throughout the 1980s and 1990s Sony dominated the mobile music market with their Walkman. Once a bulky, brick-like piece of equipment worn on a waistband, the Walkman matured into smaller, less intrusive formats. Then came the CD Walkman to accommodate the technological move past audiocassettes into the clarity only digital audio could provide. Given her background in technology investing, when her advisor told her about a new technology called the "micro disc," Sarah was immediately interested.

The micro disc was a tiny version of the CD. Sony had just hinted they would release a micro disc player that would change mobile music forever. Users would finally be able to have a player no larger than a business card on their waistband or in their pocket. The sound was said to be incredible, and Sony held the patent on this technology. They would corner the market, and their investors stood to make millions. Sony isn't some wide-eyed entrepreneur looking for money. Sony music had a twenty-year history of making billions from their technology. They were a legitimate, Grade A corporation. However, on the morning of September 11, 2001, everything changed. Airborne terrorist attacks targeting New York, Washington, and the Pentagon seized all financial markets. All long positions suffered. The Dow and S&P dropped aggressively. No one on earth could have predicted this event. Sarah's Sony investment was not a bad investment—remember, weeds just grow. But it wasn't September 11 that killed her technology investment. It was something much less sinister.

One month later, on October 23, 2001, Apple Inc. released an alien technology no one had ever seen or heard of in the history of mankind: the iPod. This new music technology almost overnight eliminated the need or desire for the Sony Walkman. The iPod was a new, hip form of delivering music via the newest form of communication, the Internet. Not only did Sarah's investment suffer from an act of war, it now suffered from an act of technology. Her only solace was her well-diversified portfolio, she thought.

Between November 2006 and January 2009 the entire global financial market crashed without warning. All of Sarah's residential and commercial real estate positions took more than a 50 percent hit, and as if that weren't enough, now her Sony position dropped to $19 per share. Totally frustrated, Sarah called her advisor and ordered a total liquidation of her position.

Between her Sony stock and other real estate and mutual fund holdings, her net worth dropped from $10 million in 2000 to $5 million in 2009. How will she make this money again? Intense scenario planning could have greatly limited her losses from unpredictable events. Wealthy people must learn to avoid placing themselves in avoidable situations. That voice tugging on you does so for a reason. That voice is rarely wrong.

Your wisdom mind travels far ahead of your intellectual mind. Wisdom knows without thinking. When people say someone is old and wise, what they are really saying is the person has accumulated enough experience, and experience comes from making mistakes. Nothing about wisdom is new; it is all old, very old.

Whether your lifestyle is based on $10,000 or $100,000 per month the principle is exactly the same. Think long and hard before buying, investing, risking anything that can potentially send you to square one. This takes instinct, money instinct.

MONEY INSTINCT

Human instinct is unbelievably accurate. I've never heard someone say, "My gut was wrong." But there is a tricky part of instinct that can seem to contradict its accuracy at first glance. This is because instinct can also represent default tendencies to make the wrong decisions based on past experiences. Let me explain.

The *Gale Encyclopedia of Psychology* defines *instinct* as "the inborn tendency of every member of a certain species to behave in the same way given the same situation or set of stimuli." As it relates to financial management, this can be disastrous. For example, no one is born understanding what a mutual fund is, or a stock, bond, or even money itself. This all must be learned. Who teaches us? Family, friends, schools, and advisors.

Unlike the natural adrenaline that helps us in fight-or-flight situations, our money instincts are created over time. The accuracy of our money instinct is nowhere near our human instinct. This is because money instinct is at the mercy of the person teaching us. You don't learn money instinct in a classroom. So if everybody is invested in a mutual fund or has X percentage of his portfolio in bonds, those activities become our money instinct. If we see our parents and grandparents still playing the market after thirty years, we are more likely to do the same. Once we arrive at a certain age or amass a certain amount of wealth, we will behave in the same way as those who have gone before us. We must be nudged in a different direction.

NUDGERS

Nudge is a fascinating word. It is fascinating because it is courteously critical. To nudge someone is not to push them or yell at them; it is to persistently suggest or encourage them to reconsider a current action. This is why I've titled the person you need in your life a "nudger." This person will thoughtfully challenge what you think you know and reveal information living under your nose but too close for you to see. Nudgers cause you to take inventory of all you assume to be correct. Once you've been nudged, everything will be processed differently. It will sound very different than it ever has before. The same words are being said, but your mind has been recalibrated to recognize a bad situation. Who is nudging you financially? Someone has to challenge the clarity of your vision.

Many believe instinct is a natural gift—some have it, some don't. Nothing could be further from the truth. We all have human instincts. Our bodies tell us when something isn't right. Whether we listen or not is an entirely different question. Nudgers develop our "internal ears" to not only hear our gut but to follow it.

PLEASE FILL OUT THIS RISK QUESTIONNAIRE

Ever fill out one of those client questionnaires at a brokerage house? These are designed to prey on the infancy of your money instinct. The factory knows what it's doing. Imagine if the questionnaire started like this: "Do you love your children?" You'd probably walk out within seconds because you don't need to think of these things—you know them. It is your instinct, your gut, your heart, and you would be offended at even the slightest assertion to the contrary. This is how you must feel when the factory attempts to get you to check your intellect at the door. It must offend you. Still, cultivating your money instinct is difficult for several reasons.

- The factory controls the money conversation.
- The factory trains us to perpetually invest.
- The factory has taught us to replace our reality with theirs.

It is very difficult for the controlled system (our thinking brain) to beat the automatic system (our emotional brain) using will power alone. Testing outcomes in the financial flight simulator is the only way I've found to accomplish this task.

The biggest challenge with money instinct is that we stop looking when we find an outcome that matches our expectations, and the factory sets our expectations so they alone are most equipped to satisfy them. David Perkins, a Harvard psychologist, says if we find just enough pseudo-evidence to prove our expected outcome, we simply stop thinking. And the more convinced we are of our desired conclusion, the worse our reasoning becomes. We develop alibis like "GM has been around for a hundred years" or "I must put my money where my mouth is," leaving our entire 401(k) in Enron stock. We want our decisions to have a rational veneer.

THE MONEY DIED

Too many people end up in my office for an autopsy. We dig through the financial forensics to determine what went wrong and how it can be fixed. But unfortunately, in many cases, the money died. The key to success is finding vulnerabilities. It is critical to use mental simulation to play out various scenarios or determine key risks. These exercises are profoundly revealing, and they immediately place us on a productive planning path. The following exercise will bring several things into focus. As you read these examples, think about the few things in your life that would severely impact you. What risks are below the waterline? What do you really fear? You may be surprised at your answers.

Below are examples of challenges I've seen happen to real people.

- Your mom gets sick and needs twelve months of recovery in your home with twenty-four-hour care, and she does not have long-term care insurance.
- Your kids go to Harvard.
- Your kids go to jail.
- The bank stock dividends you've been living off of disappear.
- Your employees steal money, forcing you to borrow to meet payroll.

- Your business partners fire you, even though you own 30 percent of the company's stock. Your income stops; your attorney estimates $150,000 to wage the battle; and you still need to pay the bank for the loan used to buy the stock.

- Someone steals your boat and kills an innocent person. His family sues you and wins a judgment for $600,000.

- The company where you worked for thirty years files for bankruptcy. Your pension, deferred compensation plan, and health insurance disappear overnight.

Interesting, isn't it? This list of experiences just touches on some of the things we have actually seen. The unimaginable must be imagined to expose your true risks. This is one of the most important things in staying wealthy.

Generally speaking, risk-taking is not inherently good or bad, but it does depend on whether the risk is above or below the waterline of the ship. Let me explain. If the risk is above your waterline, it won't sink the ship. If the risk is below the waterline, the ship very well could sink. This is not a mathematical metric; it is a personal one. Everyone has a different waterline. There is no waterline chart. So what type of risks are above and below the waterline? It depends on your stage in life.

If you are working and saving, risks below the waterline are death, disability, loss of job or spouse, sickness of a child—things that would have a major impact on your cash flow. Investment results usually are not below the waterline. As you approach retirement, many of the risks switch. Death and disability become tragic emotionally, but not financially. But your investment risk moves below the waterline because you don't have the ability to replace the assets.

Wealthy clients must understand this. For the wealthy, the investment risk is below the waterline.

When you have money, you must become hypersensitive to investment risk. This is where many wealthy clients failed over the last ten years. They did not consider how they would feel if the unthinkable happened. Your experience over the 2007-to-2009 recession has now introduced you to the possibility of severe declines over short cycles. Your instincts have now been trained.

SUCCESSFULLY STUDYING FAILURE

As we discussed in the first chapter, one of the best ways to cultivate instinct is to study failure before you experience it. People who have experienced monumental failures have adhered to certain thought patterns, certain oversights, certain unbroken chains of errors.

You must study financial failures such as Long-Term Capital Management, Fannie Mae, and AIG, but you must also study how John MacAfee (the computer antivirus guru we will discuss a little later) unnecessarily lost 96 percent of his wealth. You must take these bad events seriously and heed the warning signs they offer. You may unknowingly be suffering from many of the same approaches that destroyed the wealth of some very smart people.

The fact is this: Most of us are bad at spotting our own weeds. We walk by them every day in our yard. They've been there so long they're simply a part of the landscape. We like our weeds. Pointing out how they damage us requires us to look internally at the blockage in our vision, our complacency. Nobody likes that. This is why doctors don't see doctors and attorneys never represent themselves; they can't see their weeds. This is why I use another financial professional in our office to do my personal financial planning; I can't see my weeds either. The good news is, now that you understand the elements of this challenge, you are much better equipped to stop your biases from damaging your entire financial garden. Find the weeds and dig them up. To do so, you need a gardener; you need a nudger.

ASSETS AND LIE-ABILITIES

Sometimes bad things aren't obviously bad. Kinda like eating seven chocolate chip cookies. You can never tell whether it was the fifth or seventh cookie that did you in, because nausea creeps in under the cover of great taste.

We all have areas of overdose. Yours may be food, clothes, or cars. Don't let the quiet ones fool you. Everyone has an extreme. Thankfully, most areas of excess won't cause our entire financial house to crumble. But there is one psychological vice that can single-handedly cause irreparable damage. It is the ultimate enemy of good decision making. I call it your lie-ability.

Lie-abilities

What is your lie-ability? It's the ability to lie to yourself. Lie-abilities can be clandestine. Unlike their phonetic twins, lie-abilities can't be seen on a ledger. They can't be reduced by accumulating greater assets. Lie-abilities are difficult to quantify because they are invisible. They reside in your thinking and take the form of decisions not made rather than traceable actions.

Lie-abilities have no respect for evidence. Their agenda is to deceive you long enough so that, when you finally accept the truth, it is too late to do you any good. Let's take a humbling look at how dangerous lie-abilities can be.

Flying is the ultimate example of risk, and the ultimate example of trust.

Soft Dissent

Nowhere is it more important to listen to soft dissent than when flying. For pilots, the whisper of danger can be drowned out by the bullhorn of training and confidence. Such was the case on December 28, 1973, when United Airlines Flight 173 left Denver, Colorado, bound for Portland, Oregon. A malfunctioning indicator light falsely warned of problems with the landing gear. The pilot, as one investigator described him, was an arrogant S.O.B who kept circling the airport trying to figure out what was wrong with the landing gear. In other words, he had a high lie-ability quotient. While pilots are trained to follow strict procedures, even strict procedures must be opened for questioning to avoid a perfectly attached chain of errors.

Nothing was wrong with the plane; a busted indicator light was the only problem. The captain married himself to the idea that his landing gear wasn't operating correctly and continued to circle the airport. He ignored his copilot's low fuel warnings (soft dissent) and pressed forward. Ultimately, the plane ran out of fuel and crashed into a Portland suburb, killing ten and seriously wounding twenty-four people on board.[9] Other options were available. Namely, the captain could've landed the plane on its belly, risking serious injury but opening up the possibility of surviving. Instead, he made what I call an "invisible decision." An invisible decision is one not made by you, but one made for you. Invisible decisions are never to your advantage.

Only one year earlier, on December 29, 1972, an Eastern Air

---

9   http://en.wikipedia.org/wiki/United_Airlines_Flight_173.

Lines flight met a similar fate. The Eastern crew became hypnotized by a tiny green light that wasn't on. This light was designed to illuminate when the nose gear is down and locked. Since it wasn't on, the crew thought a malfunctioning nose gear was certainly the problem. They never took time to consider maybe the indicator light was the problem. Their lie-abilities convinced them such a simple solution was impossible. In the process of connecting that chain of errors, the crew mistakenly disconnected the autopilot, causing a slow descent. The plane crashed into the Everglades, killing 101 people. A post-crash investigation revealed the landing gear was down and locked the entire time. The plane was in perfect condition. Only the 99¢ indicator light was broken.

Many things went wrong on this flight, but at the core was the crew's failure to seek information contrary to their assumptions. While looking for the problem that caused a tiny green light to not come on, they forgot to monitor the other important flight instruments, which would have told them their speed and altitude were severely compromised, and they didn't consider the possibility of a faulty indicator.

We must always check the integrity of indicators designed to warn us of danger. Faulty indicators of all kinds can move us one generation away from what we should really concentrate on. They can be the blinding twig that keeps us from seeing the falling oak. This is why nudgers are so valuable and trained instinct so powerful. They are our priceless sources of soft dissent. Tunnel vision is almost impossible to break on our own; we must have someone tapping on our shoulder.

Wisdom is often expressed ever so softly. Are you listening?

Taming Your Lie-abilities

We all overestimate our knowledge. In Sweden, 94 percent of drivers believe their skills put them in the top 50 percent of drivers. Nearly 85 percent of Frenchmen believe their lovemaking abilities put them in the top half as well. A successful person will try to convince you his achievements were the result of skill, just as a gambler on a winning streak will. But we have to take into account the number of people who started the game to determine that the probability is not in our favor. If your reference point begins with the winners, as when you check to see which funds topped the charts last month, you ignore everyone who started the race and did not finish. Before the race began, could you have picked the winner? Probably not.

I appreciate the writings of Malcolm Gladwell. If you've read his book *Blink* you're familiar with the following story. Ted Williams was one of the most celebrated hitters of all time. He claimed to be able to "look the ball onto the bat," tracking it to the precise point where it made contact. This event happens so quickly, however, that this skill of Williams is an impossibility.

In an effort to learn more about how athletes like Williams seem to possess this ability, Vic Braden did a study of tennis players and used digitized videotapes to study every move the tennis player makes. Every player in the world will tell you he rolls his wrist when hitting the ball. But when the tapes are analyzed, Braden found that none of them did. In fact, the last five feet of the ball's flight are invisible to the players, so they have no idea what they're doing, but they are convinced they do. When Vic Braden ran into Ted Williams at an event, he asked him how he could see the ball when it was physically impossible. Ted responded, "Well, I guess it just seemed like I could do that." Williams is one of the best baseball players in history, but the reality is, not even he understands his own success. He operated on instinct.

But this is not the problem. Our real challenge is to avoid self-deception in areas that have profound effects on our money, health, or happiness. Things that can be changed should be changed, no matter how much it may hurt your ego to admit that they must be changed. It can be as simple as facing the evidence, listening to dissent, analyzing its veracity, and implementing relevant changes.

You've probably heard this a million times: "People don't change." That is a societal lie-ability. It is wrong, but because everyone says it, everyone believes it. In reality, people change every day, sometimes for the good, sometimes for the bad. But we are all capable of positive change. When presented with better information, we can make better decisions for our future.

The first step toward taming your lie-ability is to look at whom it is you are trying to impress. If we are honest, we all try to impress somebody: a parent, a girlfriend, a colleague, or even an enemy. The most empowering feeling you will ever have is crawling out from under the weight of other people's opinions. Once you stop trying to impress others, you can finally begin to impress yourself. It's a much simpler approach to life. That is what the great ones do. Thomas Edison didn't seek to impress you. His obsession was to prove his ideas to himself; as a result, you have light. Bill Gates didn't seek to impress you; he sought to prove whether this computer thing was worth forfeiting a Harvard degree for. He sought to impress himself, and in doing so, he impressed us all.

PAINTING A TRUTHFUL PICTURE

We've talked about how you can deceive yourself and the powerful consequences of bad decisions. Now let's look at how you establish a true picture of what you want in your life. Let's talk about your assets.

This is more complicated than it seems, because often we can't describe our goals in much detail. We understand what we want at the helicopter level but struggle to describe our desires at the ground level. This paradox causes us to seek solutions not always best for our long-term happiness. What we need is clarity. We need to weave together a tangible picture based on our mental picture of what we want—a kind of open-architecture blueprint.

To begin the "painting process" my firm starts with helping clients articulate their vision. I borrow a concept from Cameron Herold, the entrepreneur who helped put 1-800-GOT-JUNK? on the map. In Herold's view, before any successful entrepreneur can begin to inspire his employees, he must articulate a vision of the destination. He calls this the Painted Picture.

Herold uses an excellent analogy we all understand: building our dream home. Where do you want your house to be? How many bedrooms and bathrooms? Do you want a pool? A Japanese garden overlooking the ski slopes in Aspen or the beach in Maui? Answers to these questions form a very specific vision and guide the building process in a very efficient, productive manner. The alternative is handing an architect $3 million and asking him to build your dream home with little or no direction. If you left town for nine months and returned to your home, what is the probability your house would look like the dream home you imagined? Very unlikely.

You and your advisors are the architects of your lifestyle. Your portfolio manager is your builder. Before constructing the most appropriate financial plan for you, your dream must be clearly articulated. If you want a financial advisor to really dig into your dream, you must take the time to develop the Painted Picture. The advisor cannot and should not paint your picture for you.

THREE METRICS TO MONITOR NEXT TIME YOU TALK TO YOUR ADVISOR

When you leave your advisor's office, do you leave thinking, *There were things I didn't get a chance to say* or *I just feel like I am missing something*? Next time you visit, see if you can mentally keep track of these metrics:

- The speaking-to-listening ratio
- The planning-to-investment ratio
- The length of your financial plan

The Speaking-to-Listening Ratio

Is your advisor talking or listening? In my years of experience, you, the client, should be talking 75 percent of the time in the first hour of the meeting. Your advisor should be asking probing questions. If your advisor is talking more than listening, he is not spending the time to own your situation. Your agenda is not leading; his is. Any advice you get is going to be the same advice given to all of his clients.

The Planning-to-Investment Ratio

Is your advisor spending more time talking about your planning or your portfolio investments? If he is spending less than 80 percent of your meeting time on planning, he doesn't understand what is important. Your investments will be unpredictable. You can't control the gains or losses of your investments, but you can control the plan to handle both scenarios. Other than general commentary about why certain assets are in your portfolio, time should be spent on stress-testing imaginative assumptions.

The Length of Your Financial Plan

A financial plan should not exceed ten pages. The purpose of your financial plan is to simplify the complex and create meaningful action steps you can implement today. That's it. Everything else is fluff or a guess, and it distracts you from what is important. A very respectable CPA firm in Atlanta prepared a financial plan for a new client of mine. The document exceeded 140 pages and contained useless Monte Carlo simulations and predictions about his life forty years from today. On one page, it even said his net worth had a high degree of likelihood of exceeding $70 million in forty years, but the document missed two key torpedoes that could leave him penniless. He left feeling the same emptiness he started with.

By now you know how toxic prediction-based financial plans are to your wealth. If your plan is more than ten pages long, it requires a very good explanation by your planner. To see an example of what a good financial plan looks like, please visit www.onlygetrichonce.com/plan.

• • • • •

Keep these simple nudges in your head. You may have a "smart" advisor who is probably very respectable, very nice, and intends to do a good job, but just doesn't get it. The wealthy must implement strategies to change what needs changing, using the greatest leverage available to us all: common sense.

CHAPTER 7

Happiness

A bird and a fish can fall in love, but where would they live?[10] Sometimes we know what makes us happy but never get around to the details. Even worse is knowing the details but never making it happen.

This chapter is only three pages long on purpose. The most profound things in life are simple. They are difficult to find, and even harder to keep around. I speak of happiness.

What do you think of when you hear the word *happiness*? You probably don't think of stock charts or market analysis. In their book *The Happy Book: A Journal to Celebrate What Makes You Happy*, Rachel Kempster and Meg Leder highlight the simple roots of human happiness. They detail in part how many things create accents of happiness in our daily lives, most of which we forget until asked to remember.

These events include yawning, stretching, changing out of wet shoes and socks, and feeling it get dark outside. Kempster and Leder

---

10 Paraphrased from the 1998 film *EverAfter*.

explain it this way: It's "about celebrating what makes you glad, what gives you joy from your heart down to the tips of your toes, what makes you quietly appreciative and full inside, or what makes you feel just dang content."

Happiness is like a traveler looking for a place to rest. It seeks our attention and will do anything to squeeze a smile onto our faces. Happiness will show up temporarily in the most unlikely of places— the echo of a flute in an underpass or driving up the coast with the radio off. Both make us feel alive. They point us to a realization, a freedom that, if harnessed, changes everything.

Your greatest period of happiness may have been the day you graduated from college. This is only discovered in retrospect. Graduation day can represent ultimate freedom. No money and no responsibility, with your entire life in front of you. No strings attached. Did you know you can go back there? There is a road back.

In his book *The Happiness Hypothesis: Finding Modern Truth in Ancient Wisdom*, Jonathan Haidt makes several interesting observations. He points out that happiness and its longevity generally mean four things are present:

- Control
- Progress
- Vision
- Connectedness

I can attest to the validity of each of his points, but again, how do you get there from here? You get there by first defining what makes you happy. This requires a higher level of awareness, as happiness rarely takes the form of lightning and thunder. More often, it is quiet and unassuming. You must pay attention to the little things.

Once you've defined what happiness is for you, you must be determined to create your own map. This means tossing any pre-defined, generic journey forced upon you. In the book *Too Soon Old, Too Late Smart: Thirty True Things You Need to Know Now,* author Gordon Livingston, M.D., quotes his platoon sergeant from his days at Fort Bragg. In an effort to find his bearings during a training exercise, Livingston became disoriented. What he was seeing and what was on his map did not agree. His sergeant said, "If the map don't agree with the ground, then the map is wrong."

My goal as an advisor and coach is to bring your ground and your map into agreement, to pull the accents of happiness out of the shadows and let them lead your journey. Any financial advice, investment opportunity, or business venture that doesn't agree with the ground is wrong. It's that simple.

This book is designed to incite inspiration. My desire is that you interact with rather than take my suggestions—or those of others—blindly. As you build your individual map to happiness, I hope you can take my experiences, mesh them with your own experiences, and arrive at the conclusions best for you.

Be happy now.

CHAPTER 8

Your Point of Independence

Deep down inside we know what we want. Even if we can't articulate it, we know it still. Life has a way of delaying our dreams so long we deceive ourselves they no longer matter. We throw our dreams onto the scrap heap of youthful ideas. But if we're honest, these dreams have grown up with us, and although neglected, the smallest reminders can awaken them. Tired but still alive, they beg us to breathe life into them once more.

As if to grant temporary reprieve, life allows us to witness encouraging displays of the human spirit conquering insurmountable odds. We see it in the underdog athlete who, all his life tagged a loser, grows up to cross the Olympic finish line first. We see it in a young businessperson who with empty pockets and passion builds a billion-dollar empire with that intangible capital called perseverance. This gives us hope to follow our dreams and concentrate on what brings happiness to our lives. The challenge is keeping our resolve alive. The challenge is making that temporary feeling our daily existence.

Being fortunate enough to have substantial financial resources places you in a unique place. Not a place of vanity, but one that enables you to permanently release the human spirit we so often admire in others. But to do this requires an overhaul of how you perceive, treat, and manage these resources.

The question isn't "What will you do with your wealth?" It's "What will your wealth do for you?" Let's look at a concrete example of how powerful your Point of Independence can be in establishing a happier life.

I had one client in her late thirties. She was frugal and paid very well by a large corporation. The first thing we did was to eliminate every expense that didn't add happiness to her life. She paid off her first and second home. We saved up to a certain level so that her deferred compensation plan (DCSP), which she could elect as a ten-year payoff, would provide ten years of cash flow. She wasn't happy at the company and wanted to establish enough runway to find out what she wanted to do next in her life. She needed the ability to float without worry, and the DCSP offered her the perfect opportunity.

So she deferred enough money into the DCSP to receive $100,000 a year for ten years, starting at forty-two years of age. This allowed her to basically live from forty-two to fifty-two, assuming her consumption didn't change, and never run out of money. This provided a quality existence while she breathed new life into her dreams. But we still had a problem. She can't start Social Security until sixty-two, and of course, Social Security won't be $100,000 a year.

Let's say her Social Security payout is $24,000 a year. This would mean at sixty-two her shortfall will be $76,000. Between now and then, she will need to accumulate enough assets to secure this

$76,000 a year. Thus, her Point of Independence is when her assets generate $76,000 per year. With this accomplished, she would have all the income she theoretically needs for the rest of her life.

This doesn't mean she is without risk. Her company could go bankrupt, but she doesn't have to take additional risks. A very important distinction. The key is to know your exact Point of Independence. Unfortunately, most people are clueless as to what their number is. Even the wealthiest generally have no earthly idea. I always ask new clients: "Tell me, what does independence mean for you? If you wake up in the morning and all your problems are solved, and you could do everything you wanted to do, what does your life look like?" They look at me with the weirdest stare—this is because no advisor sits down and says, "You should spend money on things that make you happy."

FINANCIAL PEACE

What does financial peace look like? What does it feel like? Anxiety, stress, fear, hope, and prayer are replaced with happiness and contentment. When a client reaches that Point of Independence, it's like the fog has lifted over an amazing vista, revealing the most beautiful landscape. The landscape was always there—it was only hidden.

Frequently, a new client will ask, "What exactly is the Point of Independence?" This is what I tell them: Your Point of Independence is the intersection in the road where the money you need to do whatever you want to do in life is funded without your labor. This calculation must be figured manually each time. It is client specific. No template can be applied to everyone. Your Point of Independence is a snowflake; no two are the same.

The steps toward your POI are simple, but they are emotionally hard to take because we have never been trained to think this way. It feels weird to be different at first, but I promise you will quickly adapt to the feeling of a blissful existence. I must warn you, however, that you will have no stories to share on the golf course or cocktail parties. Financial peace can be a lonely place if you consider loneliness like flying smooth, without turbulence. This philosophy will not appeal to everyone, and that is okay. Some people can never be happy because they can never be satisfied. But if finding peace appeals to you, I think you will find the following helpful. So if you are ready to think differently, protect wealth, and be happy, read on.

Here are my starting blocks:

1. Don't pay fixed bills with variable money.
2. Build your safety net.
3. Invest for cash flow.
4. Enjoy life.

DON'T PAY FIXED BILLS WITH VARIABLE MONEY

If you get nothing more from this book, this is the one point you should take away. Since I love stories, I will begin with what it feels like to be in the right place and then move to helping you understand the framework for getting there.

One of my clients began his career in the U.S. Navy as a nuclear engineer. Maintaining a nuclear reactor on a submarine is a very unique skill. One of the great things about the military is the pension at the end of your twenty-year commitment. He then began another career working for an electric utility. The reward—another pension. He retired for a few years and then got bored, so he went to work for another utility. The reward—his third pension. So, at retirement, he and his wife received the following: his Social Security, her Social Security, his military pension, and two retirement pensions. Five sources of income that last a lifetime place a person in a special place. His net worth could be zero, and he could pay every bill—forever!

He had only to worry about a catastrophic event that might affect his cash flow. The financial crisis for him was a mental one: He felt bad for everyone who was not as fortunate as he was. He paid fixed bills with fixed inflows. Unfortunately, the pension is a dying breed, Social Security being one of the last relics of the time gone by. So we must take a slightly different route to arrive at the same place.

Most people focus on the balance sheet, relegating the cash flow statement to a quick synopsis of the Quicken report at tax time. But they will update the stock portfolio and other assets daily to see how they're doing. This is backward. The balance sheet is a meaningless distraction. People who implode financially rely on the balance sheet to make decisions. People who live and breathe success focus on the cash flow statement, and they abide by the number-one rule—they don't pay fixed bills with variable money.

A fixed bill is a destination for your money regardless of time or place. A mortgage payment is due whether you are traveling the world or sitting in a hospital bed recovering from an illness. Private schools have prepayment plans but never payment plans. Insurance payments are required only if you wish to keep the coverage. And the power company will rarely wait six months to get its check.

A variable bill is the vacation budget, golf outings, hair appointments, and dinners out. These are easy to spot and could be extended to morning coffees, kid's soccer, piano lessons, and Whole Foods. A variable bill is almost anything that we like but don't need. Most of my clients keep an American Express card and pay for everything on the card to get the reward points. If you want to figure out your variable expenses, review the annual summary and add up all the categories.

Your annual need is the total of your fixed outflows and your variable outflows. The annual need becomes your metric for success. Once it is funded without labor, you have reached your Point of Independence.

People who implode financially have a mismatch—they use variable money to pay fixed bills. Variable money is money from stock market gains, variable compensation packages like stock options and bonuses, or the future profits from a successful start-up company, to name a few. The amount and the timing of the cash inflow is unknown. Fortunately, the crash of 2008–2009 is still fresh, but stock market rebounds tend to numb our memory. We have forgotten about 1987, 2000, and 2002. Hopefully, the severity of the last crisis will stick for a while. Whether you're reading this in 2012, 2019, or later, one thing will not change: People who rely on stock market gains to fund their expenses suffer severe heartburn during a financial crisis. Variable inflows have to be ignored in order to achieve your POI.

Fixed inflows are items of recurring revenue that require minimal or no labor. The pensions mentioned earlier are examples of fixed inflows. Others include rental income from paid-off real estate, royalty payments from a creative venture, bond income, deferred compensation payments, and salaries at secure jobs you want to keep. A fixed inflow is something that you are almost certain will continue, absent an extraordinary event. Failure, rather than success, becomes the variable.

When you take your fixed inflows and compare them to your annual need, the annual shortfall becomes your hurdle rate. You can achieve your Point of Independence by either reducing your outflows or increasing your inflows. I am indifferent to what people spend money on. My only request is they spend it on things that make them happy, because time is an unknown variable.

Cash Flow Stress Test

There is a second calculation we run to stress-test a client's annual need. If all income stopped tomorrow, how would you fund the shortfall, and what expenses could you change? This is probably the most important mental simulation you can perform. When done correctly, it should quickly expose areas of concern. Why something so catastrophic? Flight simulators create scenarios to see how the pilot reacts in a crash. The Secret Service does not expect trainees to survive a point-blank surprise pistol shot to the head, yet this simulation is critical to their success because it forces them to think differently. When you think differently, you see everything and everybody differently.

Those who survive catastrophic cash flow interruptions have many things in common. They have multiple sources of cash flow and a safety net (both discussed in the next section). Also, their variable expenses usually exceed their fixed expenses. You can make adjustments to your fixed expenses over time, but rarely can it happen in an afternoon. This is important because variable expenses can adapt to new circumstances, but fixed expenses don't change quickly. I get nervous when fixed expenses exceed 50 percent of the annual need.

Driven by easy credit and government subsidies, the over-investment in the single-family home and the vacation home created more hardship than any other decision I've seen people make. The devastation was precise and easy to simulate in advance. If you break down the cash flow statement between fixed and variable expenses, you will quickly see the toxicity of residential real estate to your Point of Independence.

A $500,000 home costs about $15,000 to $25,000 annually to support when you include all utility bills, maintenance, property taxes, and insurance. A $1-million home costs about $25,000 to $50,000 per year to maintain, and a $2-million home costs about $50,000 to $100,000 per year to maintain. Ignoring the mortgage, which we will discuss next, most of these expenses are not tax-deductible, so you must earn enough to pay the income tax and net the outflow. The housing crisis exposed a problem that was always there—a residential home is worse than a boat when it comes to cash flow. I always tell clients, buy it because you need it, buy it because you love it, and buy it because you can afford the risk of the fixed outflow. But never buy it for investment purposes. Your home is a greedy cash flow hog that never sleeps.

One way to lower your fixed outflow is to pay off all your debt. Take, for example, a $500,000 mortgage at 5 percent. This is a very reasonable loan for a wealthy person; the interest rate is favorable and the CPA loves to see the worthless deduction on your Schedule A. The payment is about $2,600 per month. So you think, "Hey, if I make more than 5 percent, I should invest rather than paying off mortgage debt, because the market historically returns 8 to 12 percent." This argument falls short on two fronts.

First, you have to pay back the $500,000 borrowed with after-tax dollars, so your out-of-pocket cash flow is much higher than 5 percent. Second, you are trading a certainty for a probability, which people with money should never do.

In our scenario above, your fixed outflow is $31,200 per year. If you invested the same $500,000, it would take a 6.2 percent guaranteed rate of return to make your mortgage payment. But there is one stop before you make that payment—the IRS. You have to pay tax on the result of a catastrophic event whose arrival was unexpected and whose severity was unprecedented. Take, for example, a friend who owned a group of hotels with a former friend and business partner. They both owned 45 percent of the stock with an additional 10 percent minority shareholder. One sunny Friday afternoon in Atlanta his life changed forever. He received an e-mail about a last-minute board meeting, one he had no prayer of making, which of course was by design. He called in from the road and was informed that the board of directors (really his "friend" teamed up with the minority shareholder) had decided to relieve him of his obligations as co-owner of the company and that his compensation would cease immediately. In addition, the company stopped paying all dividends to the shareholders. He became unemployed by his own company in an instant.

It was the equivalent of a financial nuclear bomb. And of course it always happens on a Friday so you can't contact anyone till Monday. All weekend, he and his wife were emotionally devastated. Had he done something wrong? How would he support his family? Would his wife have to go back to work? The lack of answers compounded the concern. Unfortunately, the road to this eventful day was precisely planned without his knowledge. It was also clear from the outset that the legality of the termination and suspension of company profits was suspect, but who has time and money to wage a legal battle with uncertain consequences but certain costs? Fortunately, he had one thing nobody on the other side anticipated—$1 million in cash.

Cash is an amazing asset. It enabled him to be patient, allowed for emotions to calm, and gave him the time to reflect on the best course of action. The cash gave his wife confidence that the kids' tuition would be there, and it gave him the opportunity to turn down four job offers and start a new business. It enabled him to hire the best counsel to fight for what was right. In the end, he settled for a princely sum, all because he had cash and could move thoughtfully rather than in panic mode.

In accounting terms, cash is referred to as a liquid asset. CPAs call it liquid because it is malleable and can instantly adapt to the need at hand. It is a majestic asset, to be celebrated. Your financial stamina in uncertain times comes from your ability to adapt. But cash also affords something more than downside protection. It provides opportunity. As my friend Greg Crabtree says in his book *Simple Numbers, Straight Talk, Big Profits!* cash is an opportunity magnet. If you have cash, people will find you. Jack Welch, the legendary CEO of General Electric, prayed for a good recession because he had cash. Warren Buffett saved Goldman Sachs at the height of the financial crisis because he had cash. Both made huge profits because they had cash when nobody else did. According to Berkshire Hathaway's December 2010 annual report, the company held $38 billion in cash and cash equivalents. Roughly 10 percent of its assets are held in cash.

Liquidity can be more than cash. It can also be something that can turn into cash very quickly at a low cost. Your mutual funds and your stocks and bonds in after-tax accounts can create liquidity in an instant. Your 401(k) or IRA, on the other hand, while valuable at seventy, is practically worthless at forty. Real estate, private equity, and hedge funds all don't make the cut.

So how much liquidity do you need? I get nervous when less than 30 percent of net worth is not liquid. Of course everyone is different, and some situations require much more liquidity than do others. Just ask yourself one question: "How big a check could I write tomorrow if the best opportunity of my life presented itself, or if the worst tragedy I can imagine besieged me?" If you don't like the answer, you probably don't have enough.

The financial factory tags cash a wasting asset because of the inflation risk. They use the fear of inflation to trigger an emotional response that prompts you to invest your safety net. Why? They can't make money if you hold cash. Please do not fall for the inflation trap. Inflation is a real phenomenon, without a doubt, but its actual effect on wealth is questionable. The stories from my older clients about the heyday of inflation are told with a bit of nostalgia. They reminisce about the CDs they purchased at 15 percent. They loved inflation. When you have liquid wealth, inflation is an opportunity. Losing money on a bad idea to protect against an unpredictable and uncontrollable inflation risk never makes sense. If you hold cash, I promise you that inflation risk is the least of your concerns.

INVEST FOR CASH FLOW

Consistent cash flow is a beautiful thing. It is like having a golden goose that lays an egg every single month. I recently had lunch with a client who receives $200,000 per year in cash flow from her bonds. The financial factory thinks she is crazy to hold only bonds. They kept telling her to think of all the gains she was missing. She fought the factory and won. Just like my retired nuclear engineer client, her bank account is replenished every single month. Another client placed his efforts in real estate, acquiring enough shopping centers without debt to live forever with minimal labor. His daughter manages the properties. She earns an income that allows her to stay home with her kids. Consistent cash flow creates freedom. Let me say that again. Consistent cash flow creates freedom.

It does not mean you are without risk. The unknown finds everyone—and always at the most inopportune times. The client above lost 40 percent of his tenants in the recent financial crisis, but since he had no debt and lots of cash, he was able to steal good tenants from undercapitalized buildings with great up-front incentives. He was able to adapt. Today he is back on the road, making more money than he ever did before.

When it comes to managing cash flow, we practice a philosophy adopted by the major airline manufacturers—redundant systems. Most planes have triple-redundant systems so the catastrophic failure of one system is not an emergency. Two backup systems are in place to take over. A quick stop at the repair shop at landing will fix the problem. The highest safety comes from securing multiple unrelated sources of cash flow. While this does not guarantee that nothing will go wrong, it does minimize the impact of a failure. It loosens the grip of catastrophe on your life.

A word of caution about cash flow: More money has been lost chasing cash flow than was ever lost in the stock market. You have to defend yourself against the financial alchemist at every turn. You sense the feeling of security and joy in the minds of those who have consistent cash flow. The financial factory knows this and creates bad products to simulate the joy of consistent cash flow. They usually come with pretty pictures and Bible-length prospectuses. But you cannot simulate reality. There is great danger in these waters, so please be careful. When in doubt, say NO.

ENJOY LIFE

Your wealth is like an ice cream cone sitting in the sun. You have a limited amount of time to enjoy it. The longer you wait, the more it melts. And by dilution I don't mean it will vanish; your wealth may very well last a long time. But learning what to do with your wealth is another question altogether. Rare is the individual who understands what really matters soon enough for it to do him any good. Too often, that kind of awareness, that kind of wisdom, is attained too late to leverage.

It has always been difficult to fully grasp the purpose and potential of wealth. This is because money is overrated. This is not a popular concept, so let me explain it this way: Money is nothing without a destination, a goal, a task.

Imagine spending decades collecting the finest handmade tools in one big beautiful garage. You have every kind of tool, every wrench, and every screw to fit every nut and every bolt. There's only one problem: You've never fixed anything. You just have the tools.

Without something to fix or a task to accomplish, your tools are meaningless. But if put to good use, these same tools can acquire, fix, and maintain things of real value. Money has enormous potential, and this potential can deceive even the best of us. A wealthy man starving alone on an island has no use for his money. He needs food, he needs fire, and he needs shelter. Money can only fix his situation by allowing him to purchase these things, but money is not these things. Money is only the tool for bringing things of real value into existence.

One of my clients went through a bitter divorce and received a $3-million settlement. She paid cash for her house, cash for her car, and got all of her one-time expenses out of the way. She required about $75,000 to $80,000 a year. It wasn't huge, but it's what made her happy. Our analysis revealed that her investments had to generate only $56,000 per year after she started receiving Social Security.

After buying her dream farm and other one-time items, $2.5 million remained. This meant she only had to make 2.5 percent per year. This would allow her to never touch her principal. She has since declared victory in life. She has everything in the world she wants and is happy as can be. That is independence.

Freedom is infinitely valuable. It protects the wealthy client from the factory and its ills—ills that keep him concentrated on an account balance while his dreams silently float away. The factory convinces the wealthy person to seek things that are inappropriate for his situation. If the search team flying overhead looking for the wealthy man stranded on that island was led by a factory drone, they would drop bags of stock market projections instead of food and medicine. The factory always provides exactly what you don't need.

Wealthy persons must find their Point of Independence. You must firmly grasp this concept, because there are millions of financial professionals hired to keep this understanding as far away from you as possible.

The Point of Independence is designed to identify how cash flow can cover your financial shortfall with the least amount of risk possible. This must be reviewed and managed often. When this calculation is done properly, it becomes difficult for a person to implode financially. Not impossible, but difficult. An important part of establishing your Point of Independence is financial simulation. This is the hypothetical use of bad events to stress-test all financial assumptions.

The process of exposing your plan to severe outliers provides valuable insights—insights that can help prevent haphazard events from wreaking havoc on your Point of Independence. At the core of proper simulation is understanding which questions to ask, which scenarios to create. It is catastrophe imagination, and it adds substantially to the sustainability of your Point of Independence.

With a solid foundation of cash, multiple sources of cash flow, and no debt, grab your umbrella; you're now ready to go outside. The operative word here is go. Go on that mountain climbing trip, go deep-sea diving, go across the world and see what you only imagined in your childhood—go live your life! You can do all of this because you've taken care of what enables such adventures: financial independence. You can now enjoy the majesty of the sea knowing that one, two, or even three bad waves won't destroy your financial ship.

This may surprise you, but many wealthy clients have to learn how to enjoy life. Wealth should provide confidence, not fear. Now that you have your umbrella, go invest in the stock market or take a chance on a start-up company you really believe in. Open a bar, buy an RV, travel the fifty states, or fund a restaurant. Do what makes you happy. Do what gets you going. You can do all these things because your lifestyle is secure, and even total failure in future investments wouldn't cause anything in your daily activities to be adjusted. That is true independence. You can afford the trial and error critical to successful investing. Just remember, no surplus should be wasted on one idea. Every risky investment should be approached as if you will never get a penny back. Only then can you be calm when life happens. When you don't have to do anything, you have the power to do everything.

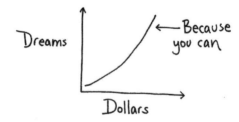

CHAPTER 9

Invincible Wealth

Wealth is a rare opportunity. And as rare opportunities go, you must take advantage of it. But all wealth is not equal. Some wealth is weak; some wealth is strong. Let me explain. Each year several people are "fortunate" enough to win the lottery. I put fortunate in quotation marks because, for most lottery winners, winning is the beginning of the end.

The anecdotal evidence of lottery winners suffering from bad investments, divorce, bankruptcy, and death is so overwhelming as to be semi-scientific. Too often, lottery winners don't have the experience, discipline, or proper financial advice required to keep their winnings. For them, wealth is weak. It leaves as quickly as it came. And leaves them worse than it found them. When your wealth is weak, people can smell it. Family and friends seem to have daily financial emergencies. And stockbrokers have tons of advice about where you should put your money. But this won't be you. Your wealth will be strong. In fact, it will be invincible.

How will you strengthen your wealth? What will you do to protect your financial body against attackers? You do this by developing your financial muscle, and financial muscle creates invincible wealth.

WHAT IS INVINCIBLE WEALTH?

Invincible Wealth is autonomous wealth, wealth that is self-sustaining. Invincible Wealth not only is powerful but also enjoys a profound level of "hero satisfaction." This simply means the wealthy person is comfortable with his or her financial accomplishments to the exclusion of all other comparisons. Invincible Wealth also understands why risk is more important than return, why confidence always precedes financial failure, and why you are ultimately responsible for protecting your wealth.

There are a few more important things you should know about Invincible Wealth. It understands that the future is as unpredictable as the past is unchangeable. It views fortune-tellers and stock market analysts as interchangeable twins. Invincible Wealth is able to withstand the volatility of a global economic crisis because of an impenetrable shield around it. This shield is created using the processes we describe in this book.

This shield discourages the wealthy from buying into ill-conceived structured notes, auction-rate securities, or other financially engineered products created for the sole purpose of separating you from your money. This shield prevents the wealthy from being suckered by a great story. This is critical because the possessions, ideas, and passions of other people can be intoxicating.

Like the common cold, toxic beliefs are communicable. But they rarely present themselves as the danger they are. Usually, toxic beliefs come in the form of great narratives. And because all of us want to believe a great story, practicing helps protect against falling for the goose bumps. For the wealthy, practicing is like lifting weights, and as we mentioned earlier, a consistent process builds financial muscle.

When you're desperate in the face of risk, you're much more likely to go all in—thus increasing your risk of losing everything. But when you're calm, you have a better chance of chalking it up to life, folding, and cutting your losses.

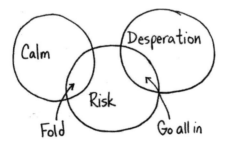

YOUR FINANCIAL MUSCLE

Financial muscle will give you the ability to resist attractive, yet unnecessary investments. Financial muscle gives you the strength to pay your taxes upfront instead of entangling your life with complicated tax shelters that rob you of peace. Financial muscle allows you to push against over-investing when you have enough money to last a lifetime. Financial muscle prevents toxic advice from having its way with you. Unfortunately, the process of creating the advantage of financial muscle is not precise. The world doesn't deliver simple, neatly packaged answers to complex problems. You must live in the present to create this advantage. And living in the present requires a comfortable relationship with uncertainty.

We can all establish financial muscle. Financial muscle is built by creating an environment for good things to happen. You cannot force fortune, but can you can create an atmosphere conducive to its thriving.

When you know yourself, you know your good and bad financial tendencies. You're honest with yourself. You understand the value of financial predictability and use existing assets to establish certainty of lifestyle. Knowing yourself reduces the appetite for over-investing and unnecessary risk because you're aware that one step in the wrong direction can easily lead to additional wrong steps. You learn from your mistakes. And one of the lessons is that sustaining your family, your future, and your dreams is a priority.

Knowing your destination is what your Point of Independence refers to. It is a finish line, and once you cross it you never have to cross it again. Our theme in this book has been there's no reason to re-win a race you've already won. But to execute these concepts requires a supporting, human infrastructure. My clients use me not only as an investment manager but as a coach, a kind of plumb line to nudge them back on course. There are too many competing agendas in the financial services world to go it alone. Once you know what matters most, and you've defined your destination, you have to join with financial advisory services who share the same objectives.

ARE YOU ASKING THE RIGHT QUESTIONS?

If you've ever been lost while driving, you know how asking the wrong question will give you the right directions to the wrong place. There are many cities with similar names across the width and breadth of America, and countless streets and highways can be confused for each other. When you ask for directions, clarity is your friend. Knowing the right questions to ask is critical to achieving a favorable outcome. Lawyers win cases by asking the right questions. The most dangerous question a wealthy person can ask is "What should I invest in?" because it will never be answered with the words "Nothing at all." For the wealthy client, it is more important to spend copious amounts of time and thought on the question "What do I really need, and what is the smallest risk I can take to get it?" For the wealthy client, your greatest investment is asking the right question.

Great questioning is a lost art, especially as it relates to financial management. And you must understand that a good decision originates from a great question. These components provide the framework into which you can pour problems and thereby elevate your chances of having better outcomes over the long haul. It is a thought pattern, a frame, and even though the pictures are different each time, there is an element of control that minimizes haphazard actions. With every haphazard action you avoid, your wealth gets stronger.

FOCUS ON THE MOST IMPORTANT THING

When you focus on what matters, something magical happens. It shows the traditional financial firms for what they truly are: fluff. If your current investments and assets provide enough cash in to equal your monthly cash out without taking on additional risk, anyone suggesting you take on more risk is going to seem suspect to someone who's focusing on what matters, as he should be. Your Point of Independence develops your financial landscape in great detail. You immediately see what is working and what doesn't fit.

DON'T DECIDE UNTIL YOU ARE READY

Investment opportunities are rarely boring. They are presented with passion, are deeply held beliefs, and have a secretive element that attracts us all. You must learn to tame these emotions. When it comes to investing, anything that must be done today should wait until tomorrow. My dad tells a story of getting a call at nearly midnight about an unbelievable investment opportunity. (As a rule, I don't make investment decisions late at night.)

He goes on to tell how the man on the other end said it was critical they meet. This investment was going to make everybody filthy rich. He met the guy at a local bar and sat and listened to the cure for AIDS. The secret of this invention was to take all of the blood out of the body of the sick person, reheat it, purify it, and then infuse the blood back into the person.

My dad asked the obvious question: "What happens while you've got the blood out of the body—how does he stay alive?" An unfathomable silence followed. They were sure they wanted his money, but they weren't sure how it was going to work.

Over the years, I've personally been presented with so many "investment opportunities" that I've lost count. Many sounded great, until I thought about them. And while a small minority of the opportunities would have turned out to be solid investments, I always give myself a cooling-off period before committing funds. What is the rush anyway?

Cooling off allows your instincts to have their say, allows you to calm down and stabilize your emotions, and keeps you from thinking about all the money you think you'll make from jumping on this idea. When you have money, this process is more important than for the average investor. Most people invest to make money, not to keep it, so again, if you have money why are you risking it?

If after you've answered these questions the opportunity still feels right, and you've done your due diligence on the veracity of the claims, then by all means, make the investment. Just make sure not to decide until *you* are ready.

INVINCIBLE WEALTH IN THE FLESH

Harris Rosen fits firmly within the rare category entitled "The Most Successful Men You've Never Heard Of." Rosen is a breath of fresh air in a world of stale financial advice. A plainspoken businessman, he is president and chief operating officer of Rosen Hotels & Resorts, headquartered in Orlando, Florida. The University of Central Florida's Rosen College of Hospitality Management is named after him. His biography includes a bachelor of science degree from the School of Hotel Administration at Cornell University, three years of military service, and an advanced management degree from the University of Virginia Graduate School of Business.

He started his professional career at the Waldorf-Astoria in New York City. Rosen was the convention salesman. Other assignments included management positions with Hilton hotels across the northeast, Disney in California, and Walt Disney World in Orlando, all by 1971. While all of this is impressive, it is not why he made it into this book. He made it into this book because Harris Rosen gets it. He understands the concept of only having to get rich once. Let me explain.

The young Rosen was assembling a great reputation as a passionate, hardworking professional when he was offered a position running a resort hotel in Acapulco; he jumped at the opportunity and moved. While living there, a new president was elected in Mexico and immediately made political changes that had substantial business implications. He made it illegal for any non-Mexican to own more than 50 percent of any real property in the country.

As soon as the equity position of the current owner was reduced to 49 percent, the new family came in and fired Rosen. It was a devastating blow to Rosen's career. This is when he moved to California to run the hotels at Disney. One day he was called into a meeting with his boss for what he assumed would be a flattery session, since the hotels were running in such a pristine manner. Instead, he was told he would never really be a "Disney Man." Rosen was fired again. On that very day, he swore to himself to never, ever, ever work for another person again, even if it meant he would have to sell ice cream, hot dogs, or pretzels to make a living. This day would stand as a profound inflection point for the rest of his life.

During the oil embargo of the mid-1970s, hotels were doing very badly. Tourism was down, and everyone Rosen spoke to said it would be insane to buy a hotel in this environment, and they had a point. Hotels need occupants; without them, you just have a large brick building on your hands representing enormous debt. But Rosen had a plan. He needed to see if he could make work for his own business the same things he had made work for his former employers' businesses. He took every penny he had in the bank and purchased a small Quality Inn Hotel with 256 rooms. Rosen figured that, if he failed again, it would be on his terms as an owner, not an employee. In an interview given to management students at Cornell University, Rosen stated, "There's nothing more depressing than owning a business without any business."

With passion and hard work, Rosen struck deals with many of the tour companies to get business. He went door to door giving out cards, asking tourists how much they would pay for a room at his hotel. Whatever price they said he wrote on the back of his business card and said, "That's your rate." When these travelers would come to Orlando, they would present the card and get the room. Rosen did this for sixteen years.

He lived in one of his hotel rooms. He cooked the continental breakfast, cleaned all the bathrooms, cut the grass, and made up the beds. This was his business, his money, and he was going to put every drop of energy he had into it. Slowly he turned a little more profit each year, purchasing small lots of land around his hotel as he was able. Rosen wanted to make investments but didn't know much about stocks or bonds. There was one thing he knew—he knew himself. He knew he was a hard worker with the passion and willingness to do whatever was needed to make a business work. So he invested in himself.

Today, Harris Rosen has a personal net worth of more than $300 million. This wealth was built slowly as he purchased property after property, debt-free, until he owned more than 400 acres of commercial properties in Orlando, Florida. On this land sit the following attractions: a 640-room Comfort Inn at Lake Buena Vista; an 810-room Rosen Plaza of the Rosen Hotels & Resorts Family; a 1,334-room Rosen Centre Hotel next to the Orange County Convention Center; and the 1,500-room Rosen Shingle Creek resort and golf course, along with the original Quality Inn property that started everything.

How did he get here from there? He invested in himself using no debt. In his view, if he grows his business without debt, he extends his runway. He creates more opportunities to cultivate and grow his business because there isn't a note due at the end of each month.

This simple yet powerful philosophy has enabled Harris Rosen to become one of the most successful men in America. And to this day, he still buys with cash. The simple instincts learned when he was the penniless owner of a small Quality Inn are the same instincts that have made him rich. Rosen is now owner of the largest independent hotel company in Florida. His aversion to debt will keep him in business and keep him wealthy and enjoying his family for years to come. He only had to get rich once.

Conclusion

This book is designed to be a perpetual window of opportunity—an opportunity to change how you view your money. It is structured to point out critical cracks in the armor of our rigid financial system, and not just point them out, but provide the fix. As you have no doubt realized from reading this text, the fix isn't an equation. The fix doesn't reside in a new approach to portfolio management. The fix resides in your thinking.

My desire is that you will use the stories and financial approaches found in these pages to forge a new path, a path where your desires, passions, and life objectives are strong enough to overcome any attempt to suppress them.

You already know what to do with your wealth. Life has already taught you. The challenge is to adhere to these basic lessons in the presence of overwhelming, contradictory prodding. Remember, the factory understands these life lessons all too well. They know how to craft very similar messages that ring true, although they are far from it.

Your quality of life will be a direct result of your quality choices.

None of us is exempt from this basic principle. If you travel back far enough, you will find that many successes you now enjoy began with somebody making a good decision. How we got here may be by pure chance, but what we do once we're here is up to us. The good decision could be as simple as your parents deciding to conceive you. Nothing just happens.

This book has hopefully birthed something else—a better idea, a more relevant philosophy with respect to your wealth management. You hold in your hands the anti-template financial philosophy. It designs financial plans around your passions, period. This philosophy says that once you've achieved personal happiness, you've won. And it is okay to win. Be mindful, these ideas will be met with aggressive resistance. Factory drones will attempt to invalidate their power at every turn. Expect this, and smile when it happens.

It takes a while to process fresh ideas. No one wants to believe that what they have long believed could be incorrect. This is especially true for those who are already successful, and for the advisors who counsel them. The idea that you alone have the power and intellect to do everything you need to do right now, just as you are, is a novel concept. It is novel because every day we are bombarded with messages encouraging us to give up the power of our happiness to others. Accepting this reality is the first step toward changing it.

As we discussed in the introduction of this book, when you have money, things are very different. The advice given to people to help them amass wealth is not the advice that should be given after you've achieved wealth. The game plan must change when the game changes. No football coach worth his salt would coach the fourth quarter with the first-quarter playbook. The dynamics of the fourth quarter are different—you have to adapt or you lose the game. Advice given to the wealthy must adapt to life.

Bridgewater Associates founder Ray Dialo believes that the concept of "following *your* dream" is a core money management principle, not just a feel-good emotion. Dialo expressed his views in an e-book entitled *Principles*. He presents the following equation:

$$\text{Reality}$$
$$+$$
$$\text{Dreams}$$
$$+$$
$$\text{Determination}$$
$$=$$
$$\text{A Successful Life}$$

This is a simple yet profound summary of the views I've held for many years. Within our context, the reality is we must resist the factory's attempt to make their objective our objective. The greatest personal happiness is achieved when we remove anything and anybody from our lives that blocks us from achieving our dreams. And lastly, we must be determined to use our wealth to bring these dreams and our happiness into existence. When we block out the noise and finally do what we were born to do, we finally realize how successful our lives can be.

Our happiness is our responsibility. You and I alone must zealously defend those things we feel deeply about. We must protect the integrity of our inner-born ideas, those things we keep neatly tucked away because they seem far-fetched.

In our fast-paced society, most people lust for information to quickly solve their problems. It can therefore seem rather corny to discuss things such as passions, happiness, and dreams. These concepts can take far too much time to unravel. Further, many of us buried these ideals long ago, and it can be very frustrating to dig them up again. But I encourage you, go find where your passion lies. Dig it up and give it life.

The financial factory rushes us to go nowhere. It replaces our wants and desires with its own, forcing us to live by a script written for someone else, someone without wealth, someone seeking a retail solution for a private problem.

When I set out to write this book, several challenges presented themselves. First, it can be difficult to harshly criticize the very industry you work in. Second, it's a bit daunting to point your finger at some of the largest financial firms in the world. Third, will anyone actually listen? But I have seen too many intelligent, immensely talented people financially self-destruct to remain silent. Given a better approach or a different philosophy, many of them would have made better decisions. This book is my contribution to that end.

The best advice resonates with your own experiences. It isn't enough to read a book of formulas or follow a blueprint if you have no personal context. Time is unredeemable. It is the only component in this life that doesn't change because of wealth or poverty. Time respects no one. So what we do with this limited resource is far more important than we can fully grasp. You've no doubt heard it said that no person at the end of life has ever said, "I wish I'd spent more time working on my investment portfolio." This is because what truly matters can't be found on a ledger. So use your ledger balance to get yourself to what really matters.

Kevin Costner once said: "One of the first things to go as

people's lives start to go down is their dreams. Dreams should be the last thing to go—dreams are the things you go down *with*. If you're left clinging to a piece of driftwood in the middle of the ocean, I'd put on it the word *dreams*." Imagine you are in the middle of the ocean clinging to that piece of driftwood, the small piece of wood that represents your dreams and passions. Don't let go.

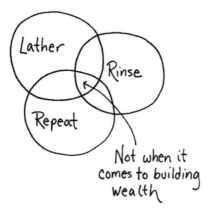

To download a template that will put you on the path to your personal Point of Independence, go to **www.onlygetrichonce.com/POI.**

EPILOGUE

Blogs, Thoughts, and Musings

The best financial insight rarely comes from stories about finance but, rather, from stories about life. The following pages represent some of our favorite stories and blog posts. To see more, visit and subscribe to our blog at www.holcombefinancial.com/blog.

THE DEFERRED HAPPINESS MODEL

You can't escape them. The "experts" are everywhere, on TV and radio—gurus like Clark Howard, Suze Orman, and Dave Ramsey distribute financial advice to the aspirational. In almost every single case, the financial advice given tells you that if you don't save today, you will be broke tomorrow. Really?

I just sat with a client with a net worth around $6 million. He could not possibly spend all his money if we invested 100 percent in cash forever. He could take no risk and achieve every goal. But he was worried about spending $30,000 to renovate his kitchen because interest rates were so low and he wasn't making any money on his investments.

Don't get me wrong; he has money because he was frugal and didn't make investment mistakes. But he was so fearful, he couldn't enjoy life. The constant bombardment of bad financial news had him pinching pennies.

Once you have money, spending is not your risk. Your risk is investing in stocks and chasing yield because you think you have to earn something on your money. Don't force a square peg into a round hole. Take advantage of the out-of-work contractors, empty hotel rooms, and the collapsing euro. Go and enjoy life. You earned it.

WISDOM FROM THE CAVE

At ninety-three, Richard Zimmerman broke out of his nursing home and hitchhiked all the way back home. He didn't want what others wanted; he wanted less. He needed less and wouldn't let anyone give him more. At last, at the age of ninety-four, he laid his head down and died. It was the way he wanted to, alone in the home he built, with nothing but his cat, his dog, and his guitar. He left no earthly tender but that of a heart. He wrote no books but the one his life penned daily.

To understand the man you have to go back to World War II. After serving honorably, Richard returned to the States during a time when names like Cougar Dave, Wheelbarrow Annie, and Beaver Dick were famous. These figures were famous for their simple lives and courage to reject the status quo of having things. Many of these eccentric personalities lived in Idaho caves. And in 1947, Richard Zimmerman, who later became known as "Dugout Dick," joined them. According to reports, his transformation began when he crossed a wooden bridge over the Salmon River. Once on the other side, he built a makeshift house in a cave on the side of a hill. He spent the next sixty-three years there.

You've probably read about canyon loners such as Richard before. But to fully understand who they are and why they live a certain way requires us to remove a few things ourselves. It's difficult to grasp how simple and peaceful life can be when iPods are playing, cell phones are vibrating, and e-mail notifications populate every device we have. None of this is bad, but many times in order to move forward we have to take a step back. Or even a step into another person's shoes.

Zimmerman grew up on farms in Michigan and Indiana. After leaving home young, he worked odd jobs to earn a living. Herding sheep and cutting wood were never beneath him. While the world grew faster, he slowed. He never had a telephone or television. He didn't think those things were needed. He decided to live this thing called life his way.

For a man with no monetary resources, he was marketed well. *National Geographic* published several stories on his life, after which the *Tonight Show* came calling for an appearance. He declined. So why take the space in a book about wealth to highlight the life a man who lived in poverty? Very simple—he didn't just chase his dream; he caught it.

I would argue that Richard "Dugout Dick" Zimmerman lived a more authentic life than many of the world's elite. Authenticity has nothing to do with what you have but everything to do with who you are. There are the happy rich and the happy poor. Money alone cannot determine either. But your decisions will.

We've discussed risk, investing, decision making, and the financial factory. We discussed these subjects in a way that may have been different from what you expected from a financial book. There are hundreds of magazines and books with pretty charts, graphs, and ticker symbols in every store in the country. My mission was not to place my intellect on the page; rather, it was to appeal to yours. There simply aren't enough voices representing the financial industry that understand why Richard lived the way he lived. And the beautiful thing is, you can live the exact same way with $10 million in the bank. It is an approach, not a balance sheet—a realization of how short life is, and how the window of opportunity is perpetually closing. Your money is what Richard's cave was to him. He built it the way he wanted it. His cave was comfortable for him, and he didn't allow anyone or anybody to enter who didn't fit his ideal for life. What a great metaphor.

Even loners have friends. In fact, Richard's put him in that nursing home at the age of ninety-three when his health began to fail. But he always said his desire was to die in his cave. And so a fragile Richard Zimmerman broke out of that nursing home and hitchhiked back to his cave, where he eventually passed away.

If Richard could accomplish so much with nothing, how

encouraging it is to know that it can be done with wealth. Wealth doesn't have to cause endless activity; it can birth just the opposite— a meaningful, passionate life full of only the things and people you want in it. Don't just chase your dream; go catch it.

WHEN THE RIGHT ONE COMES ALONG

Regret is a stern taskmaster. It just won't let you rest. Thinking about what "coulda, woulda, shoulda" is like having a nagging pebble in your shoe. Better to make decisions based on the best information you have at the time, leaving the door open to make greater decisions when greater information arrives. But sometimes our old decisions are warm and comfortable, which reminds me of an unforgettable lyric written by the 1970s' singing duo England Dan and John Ford Coley: "Oh it's sad to belong to someone else when the right one comes along." Ouch!

What a dilemma to realize the one you're with today isn't the one that's supposed to stay.

Growth can be painful because it implies you didn't get it right the first time. This need not be the case when it comes to your financial future. Markets change, people change, and most importantly, you change. Needs arise that have never peeked their heads above water before, so it is only natural to make new decisions based on new information.

Our unique strategy, which focuses on reaching your Point of Independence, provides clients with the exact number necessary to turn off the hunt for more. The strategy is powerful because it is simple, yet it takes into consideration elements of our clients' lives the traditional private wealth management firms would never imagine. I believe paranoia is the best planning approach.

Like clockwork, as soon as I've taken my seat, I'm asked one question: "Why don't the big boys use this?" (An excellent question, by the way.) The "big boys"—Morgan Stanley, Merrill Lynch, etc.— have the biggest budgets; they control financial advertisements and have influence in the financial media. Yet, the best financial advice can be found outside their ranks. Boutique firms such as mine are signing up private wealth clients who are realizing that the "big boys" have big conflicts of interest. Pleasing private clients and public shareholders is a difficult balancing act. The only way to succeed at it is by keeping clients partially blindfolded and dependent.

In my view, the more you empower your client to learn and understand, the stronger the partnership you build, and the faster you travel toward their Point of Independence. And that is the ulti-mate objective: to usher clients into permanent financial indepen-dence, even if it means they don't need a financial planner anymore. This is heretical to the establishment, but it's just what today's private client is seeking. So let me ask in the words of that 1970s' anthem for change: Has the right one come along for you?

IMAGINATION AND CREATIVITY

When and where do you get your best ideas? In the shower? On the beach? Ever wonder why your best ideas rarely come to you while at work?

This is because the creative mind doesn't perform optimally while in "the box." The box is that place that doesn't change. It is the steel cubicle where creativity dies and mediocrity reigns supreme. In his book *How to Think Like Leonardo da Vinci*, author Michael J. Gelb speaks insightfully about how one can elevate imagination and creativity to peak levels.

Gelb, in an effort to write a series of books on the mastery of da Vinci, traveled to Florence, Italy. Gelb walked the steps da Vinci walked, sat in his seat, ate what he ate, and studied his notes. He noticed that da Vinci operated at his best when his mind ran freely and unfettered, without premise.

Leonardo da Vinci's personal notes could be characterized as haphazard. On one page he would have a shopping list, under that several vocabulary definitions, next to that an impeccable drawing, and next to the drawing a stream of disjointed scribbling.

In fact, Gelb found very few "organized" ideas. It is as if da Vinci's most famous works of art were surrounded by chaos. Much can be learned from the da Vinci style of creativity. Nothing was segmented; his ideas were connected to other seemingly unrelated ideas, which in the end birthed legendary creations that could not have emerged from "the box."

Being effective in today's financial markets requires extreme imagination and creativity. "Thinking outside the box" isn't a skill—it is a requirement. The connectivity of the global economy requires an imagination that is foreign to traditional financial planning.

In today's world, thinking inside the box can be the riskiest investment of all.

THE UNINTENDED CONSEQUENCE

If you're not from the South, you may not have seen that strange vine that seems to permeate every vacant space, called kudzu. Native to southern Japan and southeast China, it was introduced into the United States in 1876 to combat soil erosion. If you drive across any Southern state, the impact of kudzu is painfully clear.

When it arrived in this country, it was thought to be an instant cure for the soil erosion that was plaguing farmers. It grows a foot a day, has a deep root system, and improves the nitrogen content in soil. In the short term it's a win-win. The problem of kudzu did not develop overnight, so its short-term benefits allowed it to spread like wildfire.

Not until many years later did the unintended consequences of kudzu become apparent. Anything that grows a foot a day must always remain your friend, or you've got problems. Kudzu has no natural predators, it's hard to kill, and as a bonus it kills everything in its path. Life without kudzu in the South is now just a dream.

Kudzu seems to be a strange metaphor for wealth preservation, but the story is critical as you prepare yourself to battle the financial factory. The factory makes a living selling its products based on short-term benefits. And, like kudzu, they use these benefits to spread their products rapidly before the unintended consequences are revealed.

If you remember structured notes, auction-rate securities, hedge funds, and indexed annuities, you have witnessed the investment equivalent of kudzu. Only after it has permeated everything do the side effects become clear. And, like kudzu, once these products show up in your portfolio, they don't go away easily—if you can get rid of them at all.

PLANNING, PILOTS & PROFITS

The last few years have been nothing short of amazing. So much has changed right before our eyes. The hubris that so often accompanied financial "experts" has finally lost some of its synthetic shine.

The template financial approach is gone for good. The best advisors help you understand how to deal with uncertainty. An honest conversation about uncertainty brings up questions not found on pie charts or in the academic comfort of diversification theory.

To do the best job, your advisor must be committed to helping you conduct a training exercise.

I say "training" because the best decision makers simulate various scenarios in their minds prior to implementation. Testing the impact of bad events is a critical part of the exercise. Think about this: When you take an airline flight from point A to point B, you make a clear decision to go with companies known to have highly trained pilots. The reason you feel comfortable with trained pilots is not because they are trained to handle smooth flying but because they are trained to handle turbulence.

Theoretically, anybody can hold the stick steady as the plane travels along uneventful skies. The value is this: When a storm arises, only those with solid planning (training) can safely pilot you to the ground. Their value is that they have been tested in stressful environments prior to the stressful event (mental simulation), thus giving you a better chance at survival.

So who's piloting your financial future? Who's drawing your plans? Who's protecting your profit? Have they positioned you to reduce the chance of catastrophe, or have they increased its likelihood?

The days, months, and years ahead will reward those who have developed thorough mental simulations. Now's the time to revisit your advisor, revisit your plans, and make changes *before* the next storm.

FINANCIAL ADVISOR, M.D.

When was the last time you went to the doctor because you felt great? The impetus for making that appointment is usually preceded with discomfort, pain, or just a general sick feeling.

Normalcy rarely creates action.

Financial advisors and physicians are similar in this way. Both are usually on the receiving end of something gone wrong. Clients don't come to me because they haven't lost any money and just want to say hello. I see the unhappy, the disappointed, and the disillusioned, but this is changing.

Like the rise of preventive medicine, there is a growing trend toward replacing financial catastrophe recovery with avoidance of the catastrophe in the first place. It's an approach in which the only Wall Street is Your Street, and the best long-term investment is the one made in your long-term happiness.

Granted, this idea takes a while to break through. The financial factory brims with opaque rhetoric. It creates unnecessary complications that only serve to discourage the commonsense answers, which are routinely ignored.

Like our physical health, our financial health can be extended by leveraging preventive maintenance. Healthy financial living isn't a matter of luck or inheritance. It's a matter of information and the courage to follow better ideas.

Acknowledgments

I have many people to thank for this book. First and foremost, I thank my mom and dad for tolerating a very difficult child. I owe you everything. You created the safety for me to make mistakes.

To my college professor Rex Thompson. I still don't know why you picked me to be in your class. My grades were not special, but your insight was. The experiences you shared, the money managers who spoke with us, and exposure to the endowment at SMU set the path for my life's journey.

To Dan Wheeler and Dave Butler at Dimensional Fund Advisors for letting a twenty-year-old wander the hallways. Thank you for exposing me to a sea of new ideas. To my clients past and present. I can't begin to explain the value of the discussions we've had over the years. You taught me a lot about happiness, hardships, family, and dreams. Thank you.

To James Bethea, you witnessed my struggle four years ago and made the recommendation to join a great group of entrepreneurs. Through Jim, I met Greg Alexander, Eric Sweeney, Miles Young, David Lefkovits, Frank Meertens, and James Hill, who provided the most insightful nudges as I was working on the ideas for this book.

To Dewitt Jones, who guided us with his own experiences and forced us to answer hard questions early in this process. To Pat Sadler for the time he spent with us discussing his experiences fighting the factory. To our editor, Aaron Hierholzer, for his meaningful work on the first draft of this book. And to Dennis Ross III, who worked with me for three years turning my struggle into a story. He took my thoughts and made the words special.

I also have to thank many authors for their works. This book could not have happened without them—Malcolm Gladwell, Nassim Taleb, Seth Godin, Charles MacKay, James Surowiecki, Daniel Pink, Gary Klein, Chip Heath and Dan Heath, Jonathan Haidt, Austin Howe, Tim Ferriss, Garr Reynolds, Nancy Duarte, Sally Hogshead, Frank Partnoy, Roger Lowenstein, Gordon Livingston, Dennis Prager, Jason Fried and David Heinemeier Hansson, Richard Hudson and Benoit Mandelbrot, Paul Carroll and Chunka Mui, Mihaly Csikszentmihalyi, Jonah Lehrer, Richard Thaler and Cass Sunstein, Barry Schwartz, Dan Gardner, Simon Sinek, Daniel Gilbert, Ori Brafman and Rom Brafman, Robert Maurer, Hugh Massie, Michael Lewis, and Michael Gelb—to name some of the many who influenced this book.

To Tanya Kuhlman for her love and support.

Index